What Wisden Means to Me

Foreword

There used to be a library towards the top of Leathers Lane in Halewood, Liverpool. It was, with the benefit of hindsight, a typical '70s building – square, quite bland and spacious inside. It seemed to be a library in name only as there appeared to be a shortage of books within. As the sole purpose of a library is, I would imagine where they still exist – to allow people to borrow, browse and read various works of literature, the lack of such works on the shelves of the Leathers' Lane library was a little surprising.

The reference room was often locked, and only with the kind permission of the various ladies who oversaw the desk was anyone allowed inside. There was an air of mystery about the reference room simply because it was locked, and so the natural thing for me to do was to ask to go inside. Dictionaries, the occasional atlas, even the *Encyclopaedia Britannica* rested heavily on the wooden shelves; there were also hundreds of other long-forgotten books, along with one in particular that only caught my eye because it was yellow.

Wrapped in a removable plastic cover, this yellow book was the 1976 *Wisden Cricketers' Almanack*. I had absolutely no interest in cricket; I didn't understand how a game could go on for day after day and in the end a draw could be called. My mind was closed to it: maybe my upbringing made me think that cricket was an elitist sport, only played in certain schools and not for the likes of me. Indeed, my senior school had allowed the third-years to play cricket for around a month in the previous school year, but abandoned the experiment when someone called McGinty was hit in the face whilst batting. Strange how I can remember his name.

In retrospect, my reading and in many ways my sporting life changed when I opened that *Wisden*. When I pick up my 1976 now and try to fathom what it was that grabbed my attention, I can't recall. I am pretty sure it had something to do with Lancashire, but more to do with the numbers on the pages – the endless numbers. It was also the feel of the book and its size, and I spent a couple of hours just browsing through it.

The following Sunday I actually watched a John Player League match on BBC2. I have no idea of the teams but I remember listening to an interview between innings conducted by someone I now know to have probably been Peter Walker. The content is a distant memory, as is the game, but the following day after school, I went back into the library and I looked at the JPL season covered in the 1976 *Wisden*. I guess I was hooked.

My first *Wisden* purchase was made from a chap who advertised in the 1978. I sent him a postal order and waited and watched every day for eight weeks as the postman delivered our post – minus a package containing my book.

Funny to think that nowadays a turnaround of a couple of days is the norm. I didn't return to him for any more books because I found a lovely bookshop on Lark Lane in Liverpool, and over the coming years my self-conscious, gangly frame would make its way to the bookshop on a Saturday morning, always just as it opened, to see what new *Wisden* delights the shelves held. Back then, I had no desire to collect back to a certain year or to own a full set: I just wanted to read them, to explore matches, seasons, records and teams.

A friend and I used to have two football pools rounds, one on a Wednesday evening and the other the next evening. We used to earn around £4-£5 each across both, and my first 'big' outlay was on a 1963 hardback, paid for with almost a month of door-knocking, which I still remember cost £12. The 100th edition! Once I had read the Leslie Gutteridge article on the history of *Wisden* there was no turning back.

Going to Polytechnic, course books, alcohol, accommodation, alcohol, girlfriends etc soon made the money available for *Wisdens* diminish, but I managed to buy a few each year. My absolute prize possession was still the 1963, but in Darlington in 1985 I did find a 1945 hardback on a stall at a Saturday market. I borrowed £10 off my friends with the promise of paying them back when my next grant cheque came through, and I became the proud owner of a wonderful 1945. Recently I acquired around 300 old dealer and auction brochures, and in one, from the summer of 1985, a 1945 was advertised as being in good condition for £90. My 1945 may have been my first bargain! My collection stalled, with only intermittent purchases through the late '80s and early '90s, but my love of cricket actually grew. Home from Polytechnic each summer, I was a regular at Old Trafford, mainly for the county championship matches.

In those days it took two hours to get to Old Trafford from my parents' home in Liverpool and that didn't endear me to my bank. When I was asked to pop in to discuss my overdraft, I was shown numerous weekly withdrawals of £10 that had been occurring since mid-June. I came clean and confessed all: my visits to Manchester, the cost of travel – I even mentioned *Wisden* in my confession. Despite being pompous and very off with me – "we wish you would bank with us and not the other way around" was something the manager actually said – he increased my overdraft. As I was leaving he asked me if I ever went to Aigburth to watch local league cricket. I said no, expecting a chat about players, his involvement, great matches, but he advised: "It would be cheaper than going to Manchester to watch Lancashire lose."

It was only in the mid-'90s that my collection expanded at a pace I was pleased with, and after the birth of my first daughter, when money was very tight, I took the decision to stop altogether.

By that time I had around 60 editions, the oldest being a 1910 softback. When the 1998 came out I didn't buy it, but on my 35th birthday my wife bought it for me. It was the first *Wisden* I had been given. My wife has a habit of writing a note in every book she buys me, but inside this was a piece of paper, which I still keep inside the book: "It would be divorce courts on Monday if I wrote in this."

She also told me that I should not stop collecting, and by pure coincidence I received, out of the blue, a catalogue from a dealer. I bought a 1939 hardback with my wife's permission and rang him to thank him. During the brief conversation he mentioned that he was off to an auction at the weekend so he might have some nice WW2 editions the following week. Auction! I logged what he said.

Finding out about auctions was fairly straightforward: they would usually be advertised in *Wisden Cricket Monthly* or there would be some editorial about an auction. I gathered up a list of auction houses and their addresses and wrote to them asking for information when they had *Wisdens* available, and that became the start of my collecting rampage.

I can still lose myself in a *Wisden* and I tend to have favourites – different years at different times. I rarely use the internet to find out about a match or statistic: I love the feel of *Wisden,* I love the challenge of finding a person, a game or a reference, and sometimes I can spend hours looking through edition after edition just to find out when a player appeared for his school: that is a particular occurrence in December when people contact me looking for a son, nephew, husband or friend in *Wisden.*

Cricket holds a great fascination for me, but I still have to mentally picture where fielding positions are, what the stroke was that the batsmen just played or the ball the bowler bowled. I am a numbers person. I like to pick up a 1900 edition, for example, turn to Lancashire v Kent, and in my head run through and analyse the scorecard, not reading the match report, observing through the numbers how the game might have developed, and only then read the report. I have no idea why that interests me, but it does.

The idea for this book came as a result of lots of conversations with collectors and I am indebted to all those who have taken the time to send me their anecdotes, their stories and their thoughts on "What Wisden means to me".

There are many people I would like to thank for their encouragement and support, not least Michael Waby, John Pratt, Chris Boothby, Aidan Haile and Christopher Lane at Wisden. I am also indebted to David Frith, Richard Lawrence and Jo Rice, and to Andrew Renshaw for editing my disjointed draft and Bob Bond for his fabulous illustrations. There are so many others that I cannot thank enough, but I don't want to do an Oscar winner's speech and bore you rigid. Suffice to say that without a lot of people this book would not have been written. Some contributors did not want to have their name mentioned, and to respect that I have only attributed articles or stories to a few; a list of some of the other contributors is included.

I simply asked people for their *Wisden* story, whether it be a favourite edition, a fond memory or an anecdote or tale that meant something to them. Every contribution is unique. I have also included some articles from the pages of *The Wisdener,* the newsletter of the Wisden Collectors' Club, which are appropriate for this book.

Like an old record, I always say that I am very fortunate to do what I do, and I have met many wonderful people along the way. While putting this book together I have realised that without my wife buying me the 1998 and giving me the nod to buy the '39, I might have stopped, and that is a scary thought. Imagine a life with a *Wisden* gap from 1911 to 1944 – how ridiculous!

Bill Furmedge, July 2013

The passing of a legend
A genius of his day
Not with bat or ball, but microphone
The incomparable 'CMJ'!

....

1971

Twenty years ago, when I was in my mid-twenties, I had assembled the beginnings of a *Wisden* collection, including an almost-complete run from 1961 that lacked only the 1971 edition. All my purchases thus far had been through secondhand bookshops and this had been reflected in the price: the most I had paid was £15 for a 1940 edition. However, the 1971 edition proved elusive; indeed, the days of being able to pick up relatively inexpensive *Wisdens* from bookshops were coming to an end in the early 1990s.

In 1992 I went to the Lake District for the late May Bank Holiday weekend with a church group, and on the Sunday we went to church in Keswick. There was a little time to spare before the service, so we wandered through one of the shopping areas where I found a shop named 'The Gift Horse', run by one Edgar Appleby, whom I knew to be a cricket bookseller.

I managed to persuade my friends to wait for me for a couple of minutes while I slipped inside. Tucked away in a filing cabinet was his store of *Wisdens* which included a 1971 softback for £22.50 – rather more than I had ever paid before. But this was the one I wanted, and I thought it would make an excellent memento of the holiday, so I mentally prepared myself to shell out, only to realise that I had left my wallet in my rucksack, which was in the car.

There was no time to run back and get it before the service. Afterwards, I thought. But afterwards, everyone (understandably) was keen to get out on to the mountains, and I did not have the courage to suggest they all wait while I go and buy an obscure cricket book – particularly as I thought some of them might not approve of Sunday trading. So I let it go, not without some regret.

Personal issues then intervened, and it was some time before I thought much more about my *Wisden* collection. Eventually, however, with a new job and some money to spare, I contacted Edgar Appleby, by phone this time, and he sent me a list of the postwar *Wisdens* in stock.

Among them was the 1971 edition – for £20. This time I did not hesitate, and a few days later a large parcel arrived, filling in almost all my post-war gaps. When I opened the 1971 edition, I found the price of £22.50 written inside, the same as I had seen in Keswick over a year earlier. Was this perhaps 'the one that got away'?

Richard Lawrence (Hon Chair of the Wisden Collectors' Club, 2013)

When D'Oliveira was selected
The Tour went in the bin
To show Vorster and his cronies
That 'Apartheid' could not win

....

1875
In 1994, while on holiday with my family in York, I bought an 1875 *Wisden* paperback for £15 from a local bookshop. Six months later my wife left me. Yes, 1994 was a good year.

....

2006

I used to buy the latest *Wisden* from a bookshop in Brighton; it was usually around half what the main high street shops would sell it for. I asked my wife to pop in one Saturday afternoon shortly after the 2006 was released and she came home oblivious to the fact that she had only been charged 99p, but speaking highly of the part-time girl who stopped pricing up the 2006 to serve her. A week later I popped in to see the 2006 was priced at £19 and the 2005 at 99p.

> Ponting departed mouthing off
> As he had failed to ground his bat
> A direct hit from our twelfth man
> A prat run out by Pratt?!

....

1934

My dad told me that he found a 1934 paperback *Wisden* on a train journey from Reading to London back in 1964. He had joined the train at Reading and not touched the book until London, expecting the owner to return. No one did, and it now sits on my shelf, 49 years later.

> Jardine said to Larwood
> 'Bowl leg side at his chin'
> It's Adelaide 1933
> Let 'Bodyline' begin!

....

1982

I was pleased when I bought a 1982 hardback at a car boot sale for 10p in 2012, but when I got it home and opened it, it was missing sixty pages in the middle. Because on the journey home I had gone on about my great bargain, my wife suggested that I go back and complain. I guess sarcasm is the lowest form of wit.

....

2008

My son was working as a member of the groundstaff at Cardiff when England were due to play South Africa in a One-Day International in September. The game was abandoned after a couple of overs, and when tidying up late into the evening his boss called him over and he showed him four boxes of books, equipment, magazines etc that had been left behind by the South African players.

Apparently they were flying home and didn't have the weight allowance to take everything with them. He got hold of a *Wisden* 2008, a pair of wicketkeepers' gloves and a copy of *Private Eye*. We no longer have the copy of *Private Eye*.

....

Oh no!

As newly-weds, my wife and I lived with my parents for three months while we decorated our new, first home. We unpacked slowly, leaving all the various things each of us had gathered when single in labelled boxes in the spare bedroom. After work one evening I decided to crack on and sort out my books, including my small *Wisden* collection covering 1970 to 1985. I told my wife that I was off on a mission, and as I stood up she calmly said: "You didn't want those old books, did you? Your mum said you never looked at them." Ever since, without fail each birthday and every Christmas, one of those "old books" is given to me by my lovely wife.

....

Building a covert collection under my wife's nose!
It all began so innocently back in 1992 after my first son's birth.

"Wouldn't it be great," I thought, "to start a *Wisden* collection for Sam from the year of his birth – something that he can appreciate over time and continue to add to throughout his life."

I had always had a dual passion for cricket and football from very early childhood when those two interests dovetailed perfectly across the seasons, and I took every opportunity to play with my older brothers outside the front of my house – football in winter and cricket in summer.

The road and our drive acted as the pitch, with the garage door acting as wicket or goal, and, as the younger brother to twins, I was usually fielder or goalkeeper: batting, bowling or shooting were rare and precious opportunities, which had to be taken seriously ... funny how one's competitive spirit is often born out of sibling rivalry!

My passion for cricket continued unabated through school and university, and although the playing side began to fall foul of girlfriends, followed by marriage and family as I got older, the appreciation of the rich literature and historic values that cricket provided grew ... along with the means to fork out for the occasional book without having to forfeit a square meal!

I hoped to instil this passion into my two sons (my daughter, Chloe, like her mother, was hardwired from an early age to focus on handbags, jewellery and gossip magazines, so no hope), and whilst my youngest, Christian, only has a passing interest, my eldest, Sam, has not only inherited my passion, but he has also become an exceptional fast bowler (definitely not inherited from me!).

I loved those long days watching Sam open the bowling for Haileybury School, in beautiful and historic surroundings, chatting away to other parents, beer in hand, BBQ on the go – totally absorbed, not only in the match in hand, but in the history and environment of the surroundings and the old school pavilion.

The pavilion housed a collection of various old *Wisdens*, fascinating to pick up during lunch and tea, and this got me thinking about the steadily growing collection at home (from 1992 onwards, remember), and how I could maybe, just maybe, look to enhance the collection by snapping up some older years.

I began by looking on eBay and bidding for a couple of 1950s books – totally stitched up by price and quality, but hey, the old battered 1955 and 1957 books enhanced my collection. It was at this point that my lovely wife, Caroline, started to notice the expansion of books in the study, and the somewhat shabby state of the new arrivals.

"What the hell are you buying these old tatty books for? They look a mess and I bet you paid a fortune for them – what a waste of money!"

Unabashed, I continued with the odd purchase, took the flack, and started to become more determined to take this seriously. The only problem, of course, was that with each purchase and delivery, my wife's obvious distaste and her consequent expressions of displeasure rose. I often came through the door after a hard day's work to be greeted by the welcoming words: "Another one of your 'dodgy' books has arrived!"

It quickly became apparent that had I been illicitly receiving pornographic publications under a plain wrapper it would have been more acceptable to her than these *Wisdens:* irrational, I know … but so is a love of handbags! So a dilemma – how do I continue to build the collection (now I was obsessed!) under my wife's nose without being found out?

A problem on several fronts: (1) it is of course visually evident that the collection is expanding – except Caroline rarely ventures up into my study (boy's room and all that) – so that can be overcome, but (2) there will begin to be a more serious financial impact on moving the collection forward – and my wife checks the bank statements with a fervour and thoroughness that I only usually reserve for beer and dodgy wine!

By this time I had made acquaintance with Bill and, along with moaning about our relative football teams (me Spurs, Bill Liverpool), we were in serious discussions about how to rapidly increase the collection whilst keeping it a covert operation. I decided that hardbacks back to 1945, followed by Willows back to 1879 and then the *Wisden* box set from 1864 was probably the best and most economic route for me … and typically, as an obsessive, I wanted the whole collection NOW – or as soon as was feasible.

Bill was brilliant at managing my expectations on access to the rarer volumes, whilst being very candid and open about fair pricing and quality – but we still had the problem of how to get the books physically delivered, and paid for, 'under cover'! The solution was to conclude cash-only deals and arrange a rendezvous for delivery – and thus over the space of about a year we went through the same procedure.

Bill would give me advance warning of how many books he could acquire, I would begin to withdraw cash on a 'drip' basis from the cashpoint over a few weeks or months (nothing too serious to alert the Ayatollah!), stash the cash in a draw in my study, and then at the appropriate time meet Bill at my golf club for an 'exchange' of books!

"Parcels wrapped in brown paper, secret meetings in the countryside, bundles of cash...is there something you wish us not to know, Mr Boothby?"

All that was left was for me to smuggle the books through the garage direct into my study while Caroline was out. Simples? Sadly not! On one memorable occasion I was caught red-handed with a box of books.

"What the bloody hell are these – are you buying '*those*' books again?"

All I could bluster was: "No, Bill has lent them to me to do some research on the history of Sam's school in *Wisden* – I will be returning them to him when I am finished."

Yeah ... really!

Well, the books were, of course, never 'returned', and now I am the proud owner of a full collection – original hardbacks back to 1945, Willows back to 1879 and the Wisden box set 1864-1878 as we agreed, and it appears that Caroline did not pick up the financial impact on our bank statements ... or did she?

She now seems very calm when my mates enviously refer to my complete collection, and just raises her eyes to the ceiling when they comment on how much it must have cost ...

... but I know that sooner or later the bug will strike again and I will be in covert discussions with Bill once more to replace the Willows editions with originals ... and that is when the fun will really start.

Anyone know a good divorce lawyer?!

How I longed to be in *Wisden*
Record my stats and every run
But regret is now eclipsed with pride
As I can read about my son!

Chris Boothby (who has kindly put together the verses dotted throughout the book)

(Bill Furmedge would like to point out that he can be available as a character witness if required)

....

1941

While staying with friends just outside Normandy in the spring of 1992, the ladies decided that they wanted to do a bit of shopping, and my friend and I only went along because he had found out that a local bar was doing an impromptu mini beer festival.

Depositing the ladies, we walked for what seemed like miles before arriving at the venue. A couple of hours later, and a little inebriated, we swayed out and began the walk back to a cafe where we had agreed to meet.

We got lost and it started to rain, rather heavily. Stopping to get our bearings, my friend was looking in the window of a shop which had all manner of stuff, and he spotted a bright red umbrella that took his fancy, so in we went.

To the right of the entrance there was a small bookcase, no more than four feet high, with a price tag of 50 francs. There were around twenty books on its shelves. While my friend was finding his umbrella, I wandered to the bookcase, and sitting proudly on the first shelf, with a dashingly bright spine, was a 1941 hardback *Wisden.*

Two things crossed my mind: was the shopkeeper aware of this and could there be any other *Wisdens,* but my search for others proved fruitless. I wandered, or rather staggered, to the shopkeeper and asked him in French with more than a hint of the policeman from *'Allo 'Allo* what price did he want for this 'petit' book.

He replied in broken English that the bookcase plus its contents were for sale at 50 francs. He was not interested in just selling one book. His English was far better than my French and he calmly explained that he was only selling it to help out an English friend of his who had to return to England in a hurry. Without too much hesitation I said yes.

With the benefit of hindsight and under less intoxicating circumstances, it would have been sensible to arrange collection either later that day or the following day, but we didn't. My friend and I convinced ourselves that we would easily manage to get the bookcase back to the cafe and then the car.

So two drunken middle-aged Englishmen wandered around the outskirts of Normandy carrying a bookcase and a red (unopened) umbrella, not knowing if the general direction in which we were heading was the right one.

It took us two more hours to find our wives, by which time all the books in the bookcase were ruined, apart from one which I had deposited in the inside and perfectly water-proofed pocket of my hoodless coat.

When we reached the ladies the first question my wife asked was not why were we carrying a bookcase, or why was I very pleased with myself, but why didn't we use the umbrella? For some time afterwards, probably until we sobered up, we were asking ourselves the same question until it dawned on us that it was quite impossible to carry both a bookcase and an opened umbrella.

....

1961

Like, I guess, a lot of collectors, my buying stopped and started as my children grew older, and when my youngest graduated in 2006 I decided it was about time I filled some of the many gaps.

I was looking on eBay one evening and saw a 1961 linen cloth for £42. It had a lot of bids and from the description it seemed to be in excellent condition. Thinking that I was clever and unique, I waited until the last possible minute and put a bid in for £50.01. I won it!

I was exuberant. In fact I remember telling my wife: "It's the first time I've won anything in years." Later, she did ask what reasoning I had used to come to that conclusion, but in my euphoria she let me revel …

....

1956

A friend of mine told me a story, and I am sure it is true, that as a 10-year-old he went to watch Kent play Surrey at Blackheath in July 1956. Before the start of play he approached Colin Cowdrey for an autograph as he stood on the edge of the field. His pencil snapped and Cowdrey told him to hold on, disappearing into the old and very small pavilion. He came out with a 1956 *Wisden,* duly signed his name across his own portrait as one of the Five Cricketers of the Year, and handed my friend the book.

....

1978

While a student in 2008, I went to Hay-on-Wye with a girlfriend who knew I was fanatical about cricket; she had also seen a few *Wisdens* that I had on my shelf while at university. We had been going out for seven months and all was going well. We had even talked about getting engaged.

We did the usual bookshop tour: in Wye there is little else to do, and in one shop she decided to buy me a *Wisden.* I didn't realise she was doing this and when she told me that she had bought me a 'Wisdenny' I was so thrilled. This was the woman for me, I thought. It was only when I opened the bag, saw the 1978 soft back and spotted the receipt for £40 that I came to the conclusion that a joint bank account was not a wise move.

....

2011

I only began collecting in 2007, and I am not too fussy on condition. I tend to buy editions that mean something to me – anniversaries, occasions etc – and I never buy the latest until at least a year after publication.

I have bought from the same dealer for the last five years and had many a long chat about *Wisdens* and collecting. With the imminent birth of our first child and rumours at work suggesting all was not well with the business, I wasn't going to increase my collection for a while. Two weeks after my first daughter was born in May 2011, I received a 2011 in the post from the dealer with the message: "This is with my best wishes, because when she gets to be a teenager you will need every penny you can get."

Eddo Brandes waddled in
So McGrath thought he would risk it
But the sledge backfired in poor Glenn's face
As Eddo really took the … biscuit!

....

1899

There used to be a dealer called Brown in Cornwall: he was a good man, in whom I placed my trust to find me quality books at a good price. I bought almost half my collection from him over the years. He wrote to me, it must have been in the summer of 1973, telling me that he had an 1899 hardback *Wisden* that had been given to him, and if I was interested in having a look to telephone him.

I duly did and we arranged to meet at a pub. The book was wonderful and in smashing condition. The bottle of wine we shared was also good. I asked him the price, fearing the worst: "You buy the wine and the book is yours." He then told me that he was scaling down and just wanted to say 'thank you' for the business I had given him over the years. I learned a little while later that he had passed away.

....

1966
Like a lot of collectors I wanted to go back to the year I was born, and while in Edinburgh on business in 2006 I found a bookshop at the bottom of George Street. When I walked in, the only books I saw were on football and I was about to leave.

The woman behind the counter asked me if I was looking for anything in particular, and sheepishly, for at that time I didn't believe Scotland to be a cricket-loving nation, I mentioned as clearly as I could that I was looking for *Wisden Cricketers' Almanacks.* After a pause she said that she thought she had a couple of those and went away.

She came back with one *Wisden* in excellent condition and not a mark on it, a 1966 softback. For the princely sum of £2.50 it was mine.

....

1969
My earliest memory of *Wisden* was my dad buying the 1969 and promising my mother that they would still be able to afford to get a new carpet sweeper.

....

Sunshine in any Wisden
The dawn of the seventies heralded something of a personal dawn for me: I became a teenager. I was a mad keen cricket follower, took the *Cricketer* every month (thanks to my dad), played at school and at my local club whenever I could, and went with my dad whenever he was playing. I loved the game and, as my mind developed, I began to appreciate the game's history and started to buy whatever books my pocket money would allow.

Living in Northern Ireland in those times meant there were other considerations in life. The one that first springs to mind is, of course, what we euphemistically call the Troubles. They were in full sway as I grew up, and they affected the way everyone lived their daily lives, but frankly, I was fortunate to be shielded from them to a large extent.

We lived in a relatively peaceful area. I went to a mixed school, our family didn't seem to have any 'baggage' from the past, and my parents were honest, caring, decent and loving. The more awkward consideration, however, was the fact that Northern Ireland was hardly a hotbed of cricket literature and bookshops. Yes, there were some very fine players and historic clubs, but I suppose you could say that cricket was a minority pastime of the majority.

It was in the early seventies that I got my first *Wisden,* a softback that my father bought for me, probably for my birthday. I can't say that I was unduly fascinated by it, but I had begun to develop an interest in cricket books and gradually the significance of *Wisden* became apparent to me.

I tried to start a collection, but I was hampered by a couple of major factors, not least limited pocket money (although my parents were not ungenerous), the limited range of bookshops and, I suppose, the other interests of a growing teenager.

Anyway, for a few years I read and collected cricket books as and when I could, including the odd *Wisden.* However, I was more interested in getting out there and playing the game, and the little yellow bible had not yet ensnared me. Yes, I knew something of its history and yes, I, like many others, fancied collecting all of them, but I ruled that out purely because I knew I'd never have the money, even though the books were relatively cheap when compared to today's prices.

As I went through my twenties, thirties and forties, somehow cricket and playing gradually had to take second place to things like work, a wife, a house and, above all, a family. There was also the natural and gradual process of the body protesting with increasing success at the abuse of it being hurled about on cricket and rugby pitches. *Wisden* was, essentially, a distant memory.

And then, lo and behold, my fifties and a divorce arrived, and my interest in the game and books started to build again. In truth my interest had never gone, just diminished. I had always found it hard to walk past a cricket book in a charity shop or jumble sale or the like, and I generally bought them just because I couldn't help myself, but I rarely read them. However, I was now to experience something of a reawakening.

A couple of years ago, while on holiday in north Yorkshire, we ventured to a car boot sale. I saw a *Wisden* (1991, I think) and the old habit made me buy it for £2. To be fair, my new wife, Lynn, bought some sort of Jamie Oliver casserole pot that cost twice as much! I then got to wondering how many cricket books I actually had: they were all in boxes which had been rather untidily packed in a corner of the attic. So, much to the wonderment of Lynn, I started to go through the boxes and, worse still from her point of view, bring them down from the attic.

I shan't bore you with the details, but the upshot was that in September 2011, I discovered I had 18 *Wisdens* – an old rebound 1894, some dubious linens from the '50s and start of the '60s and slightly better ones from the '70s, and a few more modern ones – and perhaps 300 other cricket books.

So, what next? Well, somehow I managed to find some space in my office and gradually I transferred the books to the shelves there. However, at the same time the seeds planted years before about having a decent collection of *Wisdens* started to germinate. I did some basic research (in other words, I looked on eBay and Amazon), saw that some were disgustingly inexpensive (and some were disgustingly expensive!) and thought to myself, why not put together a run back to 1950?

And that's how the mini-crusade started. I was warned by others that it was a dangerous and addictive thing to do. Did I listen? No. Were they right? Yes.

At first I was happy to try for the run back to 1950, but, as my knowledge grew, I realised that I could perhaps put together a complete run of all the years if I wasn't, to coin a phrase, too fussy. And so, working on that very basic strategy and initially buying on price alone, I set to work. Since September 2011, on a very limited budget and thanks to the generosity of others (my dad bought me what I consider to be a lovely Lowe & Brydone set that had been bound in hard brown covers when the set was new) and presents at suitable moments, eg wedding (1943 linen), birthdays and Christmas, I have managed to get to within ten books of my goal!

My collection to date is, it must be admitted, somewhat eclectic. Needless to say, facsimiles (the Lowe & Brydone set and then Willows) make up the early years, certainly up to the 1890s. From 1892 to 1940 I have very few originals that are in one piece: I have some that are complete, but disbound. Then come the rebinds: some complete in very good condition, some complete in poorer condition, some incomplete but good, and some incomplete and poor. They are supplemented with about a dozen Willows, notably for the Great War years and much of the '30s. From and including 1941 to 1947 are linens, and from 1948 to date all bar half a dozen are hardbacks in varying conditions, but better as they get more recent.

As for the final ten copies that I need, I plan that they will be acquired before the end of the 150th anniversary year of the little yellow book. They will represent the same mix as the ones I currently have, but, it must be said, I am growing slightly fussier. I now realise that the early days of simply filling a year with whatever I could get for as little as possible are over, and knowing what I know now I would be more selective. I have no doubt that had I been a little more patient and discerning, the quality of my collection would have been much better for not a lot more.

So, what has and does *Wisden* mean to me? Or, perhaps more accurately, what has and does this reawakened interest and collector-lust mean?

Well, frankly, it has meant all sorts of things. It has meant disappointment when slightly better-quality books have come along just after I've purchased a year, or buying a Willows when I could have got a decent rebind for less or the same, or when books are not quite as described. It has meant frustration when bids have been pipped at the last minute or I haven't been able to afford a book or I've hummed and haaaed and let one get away; or because there don't seem to be any collectors that I know of who I can meet up with in Northern Ireland.

It has meant getting told off at home, with the order being to get myself out of a book or the internet and do something useful. It has meant some reduction in bank balance, and indeed, and not unnaturally, some slight envy when I see others able to buy single books for a price that would cover my collection five, six or perhaps even ten times over. It has meant having to find space where none existed to put the books: I have employed a 'split' solution – the books from 1950 to date are housed in my office, while those before 1950 are at home.

However, it has also meant that, in my mid-fifties, I have a reawakened interest, a passion – albeit one that seems anoraky to others, and that's no offence to anoraks! It has meant that I have learned more about the greatest of games, of its history and indeed of the wider history of our times, because there isn't a *Wisden* that one lifts that doesn't throw up something new. It has meant that I have spoken to, communicated with and met some wonderful people, and it has led me to a world of electronic conversations – about all manner of subjects, not just *Wisdens* and cricket – with people who I have never met and who have the strangest of usernames. It has meant highs of enjoyment, excitement and fulfilment to match the lows of the frustrations and disappointments, not least the excitement when a parcel containing another book arrives and I become a child again as I unwrap it.

In his autobiography, Cardus wrote about his time as an insurance clerk when, at lunchtime on a winter day, he had the office to himself. He built up the fire, brewed tea, munched on banana sandwiches and was "lost to everything except my books". I can picture and almost touch that atmosphere, and getting lost in *Wisden* creates just that feeling of warmth, of safety and of sheer pleasure – a haven, if you like.

As I write this it is snowing outside, but I know that if I pick up a *Wisden* – any *Wisden* – I will find sunshine, as yellow and warm as the now famous dust wrappers.

The IPL is 'bish', 'bash', 'bosh'
Cheap thrills to fill the house
But compared to Test match cricket
It is really 'Mickey Mouse'!

....

Lillywhite in Loamshire

This is not strictly about *Wisden,* but it's closely related. In the 1950s I lived in a pleasant first-class county. Let's call it Loamshire. My school was ten minutes from the main county ground and I was a junior member. As there was a long lunch break at school, I used to rush down in the summer with a pack of sandwiches and catch half an hour's play. In the holidays of 1956, I was on my way to a championship match on an outground, when I shared a train compartment with the county scorer. He also doubled as the librarian. We started chatting about cricket books and he invited me to call on him at the main ground.

When I paid my visit, he showed me round the library and said the county had a surplus set of *Red Lillywhites.* There were nearly thirty of them. He offered to sell me the full set for thirty shillings (£1.50). We struck a deal under which I bought one volume a week for a shilling. Incidentally, that was the price at which they were originally sold.

The first one I bought was 1872. After a month I had five, all in immaculate condition. However, I realised I had effectively mortgaged most of my pocket money until way beyond Christmas. This left little for other boyhood necessities. So I cancelled the deal, handed back the books and received five bob in return.

I can't imagine how much a complete run to 1900 would now be worth. I have half a dozen modern reprints, but they're not the same thing. I do sometimes wonder whether the scorer was in his rights to sell the books, which is why I've given the county a fictitious name. It was also in 1956 that I received my first *Wisden.* I feel the appropriate gods smiled when I was born, for my birthday falls a few days after the normal publication date.

....

eBay 2011

A 2007 linen cloth edition: 99p and free delivery. My best bargain!

> Sinking to a brand new low
> Pushing cricket to the dark
> When literally and metaphorically
> Amir overstepped the mark!

....

1972

I have a mixed bag of *Wisdens,* sourced and acquired over a number of years from the usual places, but the one that I gained most pleasure in acquiring was my 1972.

I was at Hove watching the second day of a county match in June 1972 and the place was quite deserted. I noticed a couple of people get up at tea and thought about doing the same, but I persevered as Northants were upping the tempo a bit. The seats all around me were empty; in fact, there were probably no more than half a dozen people in my particular part of the ground. I caught sight of something on the seat where the couple who had departed had been sitting, but thought nothing of it, but by the close I was a little interested in what they had left. If it was rubbish I would mention it on my way out.

Far from it! It was a super 1972 *Wisden* and it was the first that began my collection. I only realised later that it must have been bought the same day, or at least very close to the day I found it, as it was pristine.

> Feeling pressure playing cricket?
> Keith Miller's view, "a farce!"
> "Real pressure", said the Aussie star
> "Was a Messerschmitt up your arse"

....

Our Transatlantic cousins supply a bargain

My job took me to Boston for almost two years between 2009 and 2010. My *Wisden* collection, which at that time had been painstakingly gathered and cherished through school, university and a bemused first wife, was left in the capable hands of my father in London.

In our first week in Lexington we were invited to a "meet the new neighbours" party, and yes, they really did call it that. We were dreading it a little as one by one our new neighbours had knocked on our door and welcomed us with gifts ranging from home-baked confectionary to the offer of a new puppy. Later we found out that my girlfriend's 'quintessential' Englishness was the talk of the area.

The party was not too bad and the other guests – our "newwww neighbours" as we were constantly reminded – were actually generally good folk, who even with a hint of Stepford were friendly and not too overbearing.

Towards the end of the evening it became obvious that the done thing was to announce that we should reciprocate the welcome by having a "thank you" party, so we duly agreed that the following Saturday would be our turn to host. We suggested a barbecue from 4pm. At that point one of the guests pointed out that he was holding a garage sale on the same day and would anyone like to drop by for pre-barbecue drinks. To a man, the rest of the room immediately said yes. A great idea!

When we turned up for drinks the following Saturday, we realised why everyone was so keen to be there. We were taken aback. His lawn, his yard, everywhere, had everything from a full-size refrigerator to a top-of-the-range flat-screen TV; there were stacks of DVD players, vacuum cleaners, brand new irons and boxes and boxes of DVDs and books. We found out this guy ran his own company that dealt in liquidated goods and these 'garage sales' were happening every month.

It was like looking around John Lewis, but with no price tags. Being the new neighbours we were invited to pick whatever we wanted, but our British sense of fair play and my uncertainty as to whether we really were in Stepford made me a little cautious.

After bagging a flat-screen TV for $50, which I later found out was being sold at a local store for $990, I was admiring my purchase when the host asked me whether I knew much about soccer. Being a Reading FC fan, I was tempted to say no. But I told him that it was one of my favourite sports "back home". He showed me a large box of books that they weren't expecting, which he explained had been found in a consignment of goods from a company. There were around 50 'soccer' books, some programmes and Playfair annuals, and nestling amongst them was a 1957 linen *Wisden* – not in too bad a condition.

It may be that anyone following my tale might be a little disappointed – maybe I am building this story up far too much – but at that time, for me, still collecting from the 1970s and with my beloved books thousands of miles away, it might as well have been an 1864 original.

Our neighbour told me later that my eyes lit up. He also told me (when he came over for my wedding in 2011) that later on at the barbecue, inebriated both with alcohol and my find, that I was explaining to my neighbours the laws of cricket and the "ashtonnishing" achievement of Jim Laker.

We left the flat-screen TV in Boston, but the 1957 *Wisden* was the first thing I packed.

> Jim Laker's 19-wicket haul
> An amazing England win
> But spare a thought for Tony Lock
> Laker's luckless bowling twin!

....

1957
I spent six weeks in New Zealand from December 2009 to January 2010. My wife and I married in Queenstown over this period. We hired a camper van to travel the country and see as many sights as possible. One of these stop-offs was Napier. The present Mrs L likes her *art deco* so we ventured to the local antique shops.

Inside one of the said shops was a book section, so while my wife walked the jewellery aisles, I browsed the books. Inside a secured glass cabinet sat a lovely hardback 1957. Not wanting to sound too enthusiastic to the assistant, I asked if I could look at it. Upon inspection it was bright, intact and sound.

"How much would you like for it?"

"Been there ages, love –ten dollars."

I whipped the money out of my pocket, gave it to her and made my escape, as I felt as though I had stolen it!

....

1904
I remember buying the 1904 and realising a long time later that the letter "k" was missing from the word "almanack" on the spine. I rang the man who sold it to me and he said it must have rubbed off. Naively I found myself agreeing with him. It was a few years later that I found out that all 1904 paperbacks were like mine.

....

Grubby Wisdens
My grandfather was a proof-reader for *Wisden* back in the 1930s and he used to get a complimentary *Wisden* every year. A couple of his colleagues complained one year that the books they had been given had 'dirty' pages. They were replaced immediately and the offending copies were thrown in the bin.

....

Thank you Mr Sobers
My dad told me that Garry Sobers once hit six sixes in an over and to prove it he bought me the 1969 *Wisden,* the first one in my now full collection.

....

1939

In 2009 a bookshop on Tottenham Court Road had a 1939 softback in the window with no price. I went inside and asked the young lady: she opened the display, took out the book, looked inside and told me, £12. I gave her the money and watched her put it into a nice little paper bag. I went back to my office and spent the rest of my lunch hour having a look through. I looked at the price in pencil on the inside right-hand page, and as I leant forward to look closer, discovered she had missed the final zero: in faded pencil the price was actually £120.

Imprisoned by the Japanese
And left to wither on the vine
Jim Swanton's secret lifeline
… His battered *Wisden* '39!

"Thank you, sir, though it does seem such a lot for an old book"

....

A treasure trove
On a visit to Alton to the Wisden HQ back in 2008, prior to the takeover by A & C Black, I was astonished to be shown some fifty boxes of *Wisdens* that had been returned. They had apparently been returned for a number of reasons, including slightly rubbed dust jackets: little dents caused by poor handling, or scuffed or rubbed corners. My heart missed a beat when I saw the boxes, but then I was told the oldest was 2003. These copies were classed as seconds, but most collectors would have loved them, so I filled my car and drove slowly home.

....

1976, '77, '78
Oxfam, the summer of 2004; my local shop had 1976, 1977 and 1978 all in hardback, all with quite excellent dust jackets and all for 99p each. Lovely!

....

1960
My first *Wisden* was given to me by father in 1960: it was the softback version of that year. I was ten, and I pored over it. We were in New Zealand. The rest of the world was in an atlas or an encyclopaedia: reading of games in India, Pakistan, South Africa, was akin to reading a fiction title. I foolishly took the book to school one day and an older lad asked if he could borrow it. I let him, and I never saw it again. I then took up collecting in the 1980s and have purchased copies in some strange places – in Spain, in the outback of Australia, at rundown bookshops in the back-streets; I even saw an excellent 1949 hardback that was selling in a country town for the equivalent of GBP 5.50. I snapped it up and let the seller keep the change – clearly they had no idea of its value.

....

Regrets, I have a few
Most of my *Wisden* collection has been obtained in the traditional manner, waiting for the publication of a new edition at the start of the English cricket season in April or, more recently, the purchase of Willows reprints from 1920 to 1945.

However, I was the grateful recipient of a pair of paperback copies (1923 and 1925) in September 1958 from a generous schoolmaster at Watford Boys' Grammar School, Hertfordshire, who was well aware of my passionate interest in the history of the game. The better quality of the two, the 1923 edition, was subsequently changed for a couple of linen-cloth copies (early 1950s), but I still have the highly-prized 1925, since rebound in brown-cloth boards in November 1989 by a reputable dealer.

The only *Wisden* I obtained through a private seller turned out to be something of a disappointment at the time: around 1990 a hardback 1940 copy was purchased for £25. The book had shabby covers and there was water damage throughout the contents, which adversely affected the photographic section in particular. However, bearing in mind the scarcity value of an original hardback 1940, this defective copy may just be worth more than I thought.

Apart from my very first *Wisden* in 1950, I suppose pride of place must go to the original limp-cloth editions of 1938 and 1939, bought from a well-known dealer over twenty years ago, both with the distinctive bat bookmark (albeit with a shortened handle) and the latter copy signed 'With best wishes, W. H. Brookes'. Readers will recall that Wilfrid Brookes was the editor of *Wisden* from 1936 to 1939.

One possible regret is that, in the late summer of 1967, I turned down the opportunity of purchasing a set of wartime *Wisdens* (1941-46 linen cloth) from Foyle's Bookshop in London which was being sold for £2 10/- (£2.50) per copy. It would be over four decades later before I was in a position to buy replica copies at £50 a time and secure a decent 1946 from another dealer of world renown.

Meanwhile, I shall continue my search for that elusive bargain.

....

1968

I bought my first *Wisden* from a shop in Manchester city centre. I had heard a Test Match Special commentator mention *Wisden* and although I didn't enter the bookshop to buy a copy, I found myself looking under 'Sport'. It was a 1968 hardback and I didn't know at the time that it should have had a yellow dust jacket. It was in quite good condition so I bought it for 25p, but this was in 1974.

....

2003

While watching Middlesex at Lord's play a county championship match against Essex in June 2003, I struck up a conversation with a man who was attending the match as a corporate guest. He gave me a 2003 *Wisden* in a rather nice presentation box, which apparently he had been given by his hosts. It had a sponsor's dust jacket, but as I hadn't yet bought the 2003, it was good enough for me.

....

1962

I used to be a county member and each summer a book dealer used to have a stall inside the ground. I bought a 1962 hardback *Wisden* from him, and a few weeks later I was waiting to speak to him to buy another one (1959, I believe) when I heard him say to another customer: "Can't see the point in *Wisdens,* just full of scorecards." I didn't buy the 1959, or any more, from him.

> 1960 at the 'Gabba'
> Test cricket at its best
> A run-out off the final ball
> The very first tied Test!

....

1978

My school didn't play cricket for years, but when a new PE teacher joined he not only got us to play it but he also arranged a game against another school. We were a comprehensive in Stoke-on-Trent, not exactly the centre of the cricketing world, and back in 1978 when this match took place it wasn't really usual for parents to turn up to watch, but my granddad did.

My parents were both at work, so after school he came along to watch me bat at number seven, score three, bowl two overs that included a few no-balls and at least two wides, almost make a catch and jump in excitement when I ran out one of their players with a throw that was actually aimed at the other end. A few days after the match, which we lost, he bought me a 1978 *Wisden.* I still have it.

> Cricketers in penury
> They need financial backing
> So this bloke creates 'World Series'
> – The Establishment sent 'Packing'!

....

1964

My dad bought me my first *Wisden,* a 1964 hardback. He taught me to cover up the totals on the scorecards and add up the batsmen's scores and extras in my head. He never once told me off if I got it wrong, but he smiled a beamer when I got it right.

My grandfather was an avid *Wisden* collector, with a collection from 1864 through to 1952. When he died some of the older editions were sold, but over time I have filled the gaps and tried to complete the set. My grandfather did not care much for one-day cricket and once told me that *Wisden* had "polluted" the almanack with "such trivia".

....

2012

My first *Wisden* was the 2012, because my grandson is mentioned. I signed him up for the Wisden Collectors' Club and he has since acquired a 2005 and a book on Fred Trueman courtesy of the club website.

> For years they took a moral stance
> And if you weren't born a 'Tyke'
> They didn't care how good you were
> They'd simply tell you, 'on yer bike'!

....

John's journey
Imagine, if you will, that it is 1864.

A Victorian gentleman has just forked out his shilling, no mean sum at that time, to acquire his copy of a new publication, a flimsy paperback entitled *The Cricketer's Almanack* published by John Wisden and Co, and he has been told his purchase will be worth £35,000 in 150 years' time.

Think about it, for when you look at your 2013 *Wisden,* if somebody were to tell you it will be worth £35 million in a similar timespan, would you believe them? Of course, this is a hypothetical question, but the numbers are of the same order!

The period in which the game came to me was rich in cricket talent for England: they were the unofficial world champions. It is still impossible to argue otherwise on that point, and for me, a little Surrey boy, it was the county's period of utter domination of the championship in the middle of the last century.

My passion for the game led to me receiving a copy of the 1958 *Wisden* hardback in my last year at school. Cricket's great historian, its constant shadow for almost a century at that time, had touched base with another inevitable collector. This much treasured possession took pride of place on my meagre bookshelves alongside a copy of H. S. Altham's beautiful *A History of Cricket* and R. L. Stevenson's *Treasure Island.* It looked down on my *Eagle* annuals and a growing number of P. G. Wodehouse and George Orwell novels.

The collection bug has always been my companion, but we were a poor family in the immediate postwar years, and although aware of the significance of *Wisdens* past, my access to the funding necessary to take advantage of this knowledge was sadly lacking.

That first *Wisden,* the 1958, disappeared during my removal from England to Australia in 1965, and the bug did not reclaim me until the purchase of a 1980 linen to remind me of England's triumphant tour of the antipodes in 78-79.

You can mentally calculate that my playing days were coming to a close by then, but a fervour for the game remained. It has never dimmed, and a desire to relive some of the euphoria of the Surrey and England era of my youth took me, on a trip to England, into a little bookshop near my childhood home and culminated in the purchase of linen-backed issues of the seven *Wisdens* that detailed the wonderful years of Surrey's dominance. My wife, an Australian lady of true Scottish decent – she was a Wallace – frowned at the extravagance, but she knew what the game meant to me and thus the bug was temporarily satisfied.

Throughout the 1990s more almanacks appeared: there was the annual purchase, of course, and long searches commenced through secondhand bookshops. The subtle distinction between hardbacks, facsimiles and linen covers were lost on me at that time. My youngest son found three beautiful hardbacks from the 1980s cast off by a library and he generously gave them to me. Then on another trip to England a secondhand book shop yielded a 1950 for five quid. The gaps began to diminish through brash displays of affluence whenever the occasion demanded.

My guardian angel (the Wallace) died in 2003 and so the last sensible constraint on what was becoming a consuming obsession disappeared. Grieving can take one down many dark alleyways, and it did, but the bug emerged triumphant and eventually took over.

Wisdens of past years began arriving from many sources. The treasures are, of course, the bargains. An example was two years ago finding a beautiful hardback on a stall at a Sunday morning market for five Australian dollars – that's about three pounds. Then the Willows company got in touch and filled many gaps for me. My two dealers did the rest. Now upgrading has begun. The linen-backs are fast disappearing from my shelves. It is a waiting game, as good-quality hardbacks do not come readily to hand: one needs to be known and understood by a couple of reputable dealers if lasting, meaningful and pleasing acquisitions are to be made. In that respect I have been most fortunately served.

My objectives are three-fold. The Lowe & Brydone facsimiles of the first fifteen are superbly produced to match the originals and thus meet my criteria. Given the print run for the originals was so small, that they were paperbacks and probably insignificantly regarded in their own era, it is likely that very few of them remain. Of those that do, most of them will be rebinds with severely trimmed edges, and so over time the Lowe & Brydone facsimiles will take their rightful place as valuable parts of a collection. My preference is furthered by the fact that being paperbacks they are a genuine replica of the originals.

From 1879 to 1899, facsimile paperbacked rebinds or originals will be my target. Some may be trimmed but only of necessity. Already in my possession is a delightful 1890 trimmed and bearing a good-quality paperback facsimile cover. It contains George Lohmann's autograph.

My 1896 is an original paperback and is said to have once been the property of a London veterinary, one Gerald Plumbly (see *Wisden* 2011 Obituaries). He was a gentleman who attended the Palace in his professional capacity as well as being urgently called to a less likely palace (in Soho) to assist a scantily clad and distressed lady detach herself from a boa constrictor. We *Wisden* collectors are a gallant breed!

Of all my *Wisdens,* the 1958 remains my favourite with its faithful story of the monumental 411 partnership by May and Cowdrey against the West Indies, and three Surrey men amongst the five Cricketers of the Year. Happily a "good as new", "lovely" etc hardback copy to replace my long-lost original is soon to arrive. From 1900 on, my plan is to obtain hardback originals described by the dealers in similar phraseology to that used for my favourite issue!

The pinnacle of achievement would be a full set of originals with hardbacks from 1896. It is unlikely to occur now with the rapidly escalating *Wisden* prices and Father Time nibbling at my ankles, but the journey is still great fun and it is not over yet. It has led to me meeting some delightful people and put purpose back into my life at a time when it was sorely needed.

> John Wisden, "Little Wonder"
> An 'all rounder' of renown
> But of course he's best remembered
> For the best cricket tome in town!

....

1940
My favourite *Wisden* is the 1940 my wife bought me on my 30th birthday in 1990. It fascinates me that the third day of the Surrey v Lancashire match on September 1 was abandoned "owing to Crisis". But to my embarrassment I didn't realise when I first received it that eight-ball overs were used in the county championship, so I was lauding the county batsmen for their incredible scoring rates.

....

A carpet salesman in Afghanistan

While stationed in Afghanistan in 2009, I often had plenty of time on my hands, and wandering the streets was usually not an option. It was decided that a small number of local tradesmen would be allowed in to our barracks, and with little else to do it was interesting to meet them and chat.

One particular man had a folder full of photographs of the different cloths he had and examples of carpets, napkins, table-cloths and such. On one occasion, not really listening to my argument that anything I bought would have to be very small, as carrying a 12ft x 12ft carpet home was not an option, he eventually realised that he wasn't going to make a sale from what he had, so began to tell me about his cousin who sold books and stationary.

In perfect English, he gave me a whole list of books from memory, covering what seemed like hundreds of authors. As he finished rattling through title after title, one of my friends asked whether he had a list. The chap pointed to his head and smiled. He must have spoken for five minutes, mentioning book after book after book, and in awe, I asked him to bring along a few from Len Deighton or Dick Francis. He smiled knowingly: it seemed my choices were good.

A week later he came back and inside his satchel were seven books, a mixture from both authors. All paperbacks, all in quite good condition, and all for what transpired was the equivalent of around 10p each. After I paid him, he brought out a small brown notepad and told me that this was for my friend – the list, he said. I asked if I could take it away and he nodded.

Inside this notebook in quite beautiful handwriting there was a list of literally thousands of books, not in any particular order, and some had small pencil marks next to them: later I found out that these were "sold". I read through the list and found two books that actually made me feel deeply homesick. They were described thus:

> Cricket Wisden book, 1979, brown, Very Hardback
> Cricket Wisden book, 1981, brown, Very Hardback

I began to think of all the things most people start to miss about home a few days before they come back off holiday, but for me it would be a few months before I was going home. Cricket, Saracens, the pub, the wife, my sons – not in that order, obviously.

The next time I saw him I asked to buy the two *Wisdens* – well, I actually pointed to them on the list, and a few days later he brought them to me. I paid 50p each. I wasn't a collector but they gave me a link to home. He came back to the barracks a couple more times, but after an incident the policy was stopped and my bookseller didn't return.

....

Tranmere Rovers 250 Wisden 4
I attended an auction back in 1991. I was primarily after some football
programmes. In a box of 250 assorted Tranmere Rovers programmes from the
1970s that I won, I found four *Wisden* hardbacks for 1956, 1957, 1958 and
1959. They were in lovely condition and have been looked at far more than the
TRFC programmes.

....

Thou shalt not be outbid
A few years ago I was becoming obsessive about the *Wisdens* for sale on an
online auction site. Once I discovered that they were available I went a bit mad,
buying twenty or so in a matter of weeks. Looking back, I paid way over the
normal price, and even now I could get some of the same editions for less
through other sources.

I stopped after I was outbid in a 'battle' for a 1972 hardback. I knew the auction
was ending at a certain time, so an hour or so before I put in a bid. Within a few
minutes I was outbid and so I bid again. This went on until a few seconds from
the finish when I was outbid, and the book went for £71 (plus p&p). Initially I
was gutted, and I don't know why but I looked at the bid history. The same
bidder had been out-bidding me: he must have wanted the 1972 badly, I
thought.

The next morning I received an email from the seller with a second-chance offer. I knew these things existed but I'd never received one. On the train to work I was just chatting to my 'train friend' – I chatted to this guy for over a year and never knew his name – and knowing he sold quite a lot of things on eBay I related my story. He basically said that it didn't seem right and he advised me before I accepted the second-chance offer to have a look at the winning bidders' feedback and buyer history. The look of bemusement on my face told him that I didn't have a clue what he was on about, so he explained how.

That evening I did as he suggested: the bidder who had won the auction had a feedback score of 40-odd, and over half the comments were from the seller who had offered me the 'second chance'. The bid history of the bidder suggested that he was an active supporter of this seller. When I told my 'train friend' he advised me not to accept the second chance, and he explained why.

Basically, two people are working together to drive up the price, the bidder went too high and I didn't respond, so I got offered a second chance. I learnt that the practice is called 'shill-bidding'. I felt cheated. I haven't used any such site since

[Nowadays, auction sites are very protective towards buyers and it is now very difficult to 'shill-bid' as was the case here. There are many rules and regulations in place that forbid this type of action.]

....

1965
Mothers-in-law, mainly thanks to comedians like Les Dawson, are often given a bad press, but I can't fault mine. She has bought me a *Wisden* ever since I married her eldest daughter. The first one she bought me was the 1965, the year I was born. She also makes a fabulous Sunday roast, which is more than can be said for her otherwise perfect eldest daughter.

....

1977
My grandfather bought me a *Wisden* on my seventh birthday in 1977; it was the 1976 edition and he then bought me each new one until he passed away in 1989. We each had a copy and he would guide me through it, explaining what was what. My dad thought he (his father) was daft, and when granddad passed away my dad gave me his collection.

Although my dad thought his own father daft, he took over the mantle and to this day he buys me the new *Wisden* every year. Could I be the only *Wisden* collector with a collection from 1929 to 2013 who has never bought a single one?

The statement made by Mr Greig
Was provocative and novel
But it backfired unbelievably
And it was 'he' who had to 'grovel'!

....

My school speech day has a lot to answer for

I started collecting in the mid-'80s at the tender age of 14. The first one I bought was a 1984 edition with the proceeds of a prize at our school speech day and as such remains unique to me because it has my old school crest stamped on the front. The lady giving out the prizes whispered to me: "Goodness – that's a big book. It's going to take ages to read." Little did she know that I'd already read it, as it never left my side for the month before. I didn't realise it would set me on a quest which ended earlier this year when I completed a full set of postwar *Wisdens.*

In those pre-internet days you were reliant on good booksellers nearby. I bought most of mine from two very good bookshops in Stamford, Lincs, along with a few from local book fairs. One woman was delighted to sell me the 1976, 1977 and 1978 editions in the same afternoon and as such gave me a 20% discount which was very welcome. I also remember blowing my entire holiday money stash on three editions in Stow-on-the-Wold on the way down to Devon one year.

My collection has survived two major crises – my first marriage where my ex-wife insisted they were buried somewhere in the back of a cupboard, and a huge car repair bill which meant me offering it to a local bookseller (it consisted at that stage of every edition since 1969 and he offered me less than £100, but thankfully I turned his offer down).

Since remarrying, the present Mrs Hull has been very good at indulging my hobby. She knows roughly what to pay and where to buy, and virtually every birthday and Christmas involves a familiar looking book shape being presented to me by the children, accompanied by tales of near misses on eBay.

Perhaps the most welcome gift was a 1947 edition which got me through a few days' stay in hospital a couple of years ago. In fact I think the only *Wisden* I have which wasn't bought from a bookshop, bookseller or eBay was a 1955 edition given to me by a family friend in exchange for a decent bottle of claret. I think we both thought we got a good deal out of that one.

Anyway, that's my tale. I'm not sure how many more old *Wisdens* I'll get now, due to the cost of prewar editions, but I am always on the lookout for bargains.

I will finish with details of my favourite *Wisden* – a well-thumbed 1972 edition with a red-ink cover which ticks all my *Wisden* boxes. A good tour by the MCC (2-0 Ashes win in Australia), decent articles (including an account of Denis Compton's 1947 season), an excellent one-day final (Asif Iqbal nearly winning the game for Kent until a great catch by Jack Bond), the usual eccentric picks by England's Test selectors (Richard Hutton, John Jameson, Alan Ward) and the Test debuts of none other than Rod Marsh, Greg Chappell, Dennis Lillee, Sunil Gavaskar, Bob Willis and Imran Khan. That's one edition I'll have to replace at some stage, I think.

....

Auction fever
I live near Leicester and one Saturday morning I decided to go to an auction that I'd seen advertised at a hotel in the hope of getting a couple of Willows reprints. I was outbid both times by a dealer at the back of the room. As I wandered out someone tapped me on the shoulder and gave me a business card: he told me that he had both editions available for less than he'd just won them for. He was the one who had outbid me and I got both for £50 each in the end – 1930 and 1931 softback reprints.

I have never found a 1916 or an 1864 at my local village fete, but I did find a 1982 hardback without its dust jacket for 10p.

Beefy's 'onomatopoeic' bat
Hear the 'whacks' and 'biffs' and 'crashes'
It's Headingley 1981
And the start of 'Botham's Ashes'!

....

1970
My father worked as a miner in South Wales for 35 years; he loved his cricket and when he died in 1994 I inherited his *Wisden* collection. The most-thumbed was the 1970. Glamorgan had won the Championship in 1969 and remained undefeated in doing so, but it is the note at the top of page 728 that sums up my father: "Allun born and we won."

Glamorgan had beaten Hertfordshire in the Gillette Cup – and he was right, I was born on that day!

....

What's mine might not be yours

I am one of those lucky ones – one of the 222 known to the Wisden Collectors' Club who have a complete set of *Wisdens.*

I first started collecting, along with my brother, in the late 1950s, and there were occasional fraternal disputes over who actually owned each copy as we built up a shared collection. One of the first *Wisdens* we owned, the 1954 edition, is now in my bookcase, complete with Bill Edrich's autograph inside.

The problem of who owned which year was solved when my brother, fresh from the success of *Jesus Christ Superstar*, invested £750 to buy a complete set of his own. Those were the days! That meant by default the original collection, by now comprising perhaps 25 editions, was all mine, and from then on I built it up year on year with the new edition and, occasionally when money allowed and the right one appeared in a secondhand bookshop, buying an older edition to fit into the left-hand end of my *Wisden* bookshelf. By the time I was nearing 40, I had a complete postwar run, and one or two wartime and prewar editions as well.

Then for my 40th birthday, my brother – kind, generous and loving soul that he is, whatever anybody else may say – gave me original copies of all the editions I did not already possess. So I now have a complete collection, almost all of it in good nick, and practically all in hardback, but a bit of a mongrel in that some are rebound and some are not.

There's still a bit of work to be done improving a few editions, but what's there right now is all complete and all original. Since that far-off birthday, I have of course added a new edition each year, along with the complete set of *Wisden Australia* (a very underrated book which I thought deserved to succeed), two *Wisden* indexes (indices?) and several *Wisden* anthologies, a couple of which I have edited. *The Wisden Collector's Guide* was published in 2011 and *Wisden on India* in 2012, both books which I had a hand in compiling. I'm working on another anthology now.

Wisden is known as the Cricketers' Bible, but what does that little phrase really mean? For twenty years or so I was one of the compilers of a book called *British Hit Singles,* which came to be described as the Bible of the Music Industry, so I suppose I ought to know better than most. Actually, it usually just means lazy journalism, a quick way to describe the almost indescribable.

But *Wisden,* like the Bible, sums up for believers the true and complete history of the game, and within its millions of words it conveys the values of cricket, its saints and its sinners and even its miracles (Headingley 1981, Old Trafford 1956, Edgbaston 2005 etc). When the *Wisden* aficionado settles down in an armchair to read the lesson for today, he (or she) is reaffirming not just a love for the game, more a consuming passion, by devouring every minute detail of cricketers who played in far-off seasons in the sun.

That's what *Wisden* means to me.
Jonathan Rice

> England's batting was in trouble
> They were being bought to heel
> Time to introduce the 'bank clerk'
> In the shape of David Steele!

....

1949

When I was young my father would decide where the family went on holiday and he would base his decision on provincial cricket grounds of interest. We stayed in, amongst others, places near Arundel, Canterbury, Derby, Chelmsford, Folkestone and Hove. Dad would take me off to the cricket while mum and my sister would shop, sightsee or spend time at the seaside. He would love to find bookshops either at the ground or nearby, and on one visit to Canterbury he was delighted to find someone selling cricket books and in particular a couple of *Wisdens*. So at lunch we wandered down to have a closer look

Dad was tall, well-built and could be, when it suited him, quite pompous, and he became agitated when he couldn't get a good price for the *Wisden* he was after. He stared at the poor man and delivered the line: "Do you know who I am? The rest of the committee will hear of this." A little shaken, the man gave dad the price he wanted – a mere two shillings for a 1949 hardback in what looked to me to be in very good condition. We walked slowly away, dad tall and somewhat overbearing, muttering. As soon as we were out of sight, he said we were leaving. As we left the ground he began to tell me all about Bradman, The Invincibles, Compton and Edrich *et al.* He was in his element, animated, and I was captivated by him.

> Bradman's last Test innings
> And at last a batting flaw
> That's why a cricket fan's pin number
> Will be 'ninety-nine nine four'!

....

My love affair with Wisden and how it started

The year is 1950. India is proclaimed a republic, Ho Chi Minh's North Vietnam regime is recognised by Moscow and Peking, Communist North Korea invades the South and British troops join the conflict. At home, petrol rationing ends and fuel prices rise to three shillings a gallon, the *Eagle* comic is launched and *Sainsbury's* first self-service store opens in Croydon.

On the sporting front, US footballers beat England 1-0 in the World Cup and the popular West Indian cricket tourists defeat the home side 3-1. Above everything else, a six-year-old schoolboy is introduced to his first-ever copy of *Wisden Cricketers' Almanack,* the 1950 87th edition.

I suppose I must have been a precocious talent in those far-off days, as I remember being taken to watch various games in the locality of north Hertfordshire, and being allowed to knock up with some of the players, which included my father.

Dad had also built up a small collection of the almanack during the thirties, but he was misguided enough to donate them all to the wartime paper recycling scheme at the opening of hostilities in '39. I never let him forget this error of judgment, although he did take on the responsibility of supplying the household with subsequent editions until I took over in the mid-sixties. In more recent times, the growing collection has been considerably extended to include the Willows reprints.

The *Wisden* collection in Bishop Auckland, County Durham, in June 2009 includes 1920-24, 1926-31 hardback reprints, a rebound paper 1925 original, two linen original 1938-39 copies and a reprint run from 1940-45 on the top left shelf. The top right shelf contains original linen covers for the postwar period 1946-64. The remaining shelves carry hardback copies, in laminated dust jackets, from 1965 until 2009.

Inevitably, my favourite edition has to be that very first one in 1950. Even to a very small boy, the book had an attractive cover and the limp version was unusually tactile, quite apart from its distinctive smell! I was well and truly hooked, and the copy was read from cover to cover on numerous occasions. Perhaps I was fortunate to possess a reading age in excess of my years, but *Wisden* provided every incentive to study further and, in common with other youthful enthusiasts, it also taught me geography, history and arithmetic.

The 87th edition carried a Tribute to Hutton, my favourite cricketer of the time, and I followed his career with interest until his retirement a few years later. Already, I knew of his monumental 364 at The Oval in August 1938, against the formidable Aussies. The county championship reports were studied in depth after a scrutiny of the individual player portraits, cricket ground plans and the season's averages. My favourite counties were Somerset and Yorkshire, but all sections of the publication were eagerly devoured on most days. A wonderful, life-long hobby had been successfully launched!

Through time, this much-loved book fell to bits, despite numerous attempts at repairing the contents. However, it is still extant and is, at the time of writing, in the safe custody of my son in Oxfordshire, along with other early rejects which have been replaced by linen versions in much better condition.

If I have one small regret, it's that I failed to achieve a mention in *Wisden* despite a useful playing career spanning 30 seasons, which included four full years in the Watford Boys' GS 1st XI (1958-61). If only the master-in-charge had sent in those annual reports, as his successors did in later years. No matter, as I continue to enjoy following the Great Game, both live and on Sky, and I shall look forward to meeting other like-minded folk through the Wisden Collectors' Club in the future.

> Who is the greatest sportsman ever?
> Well, a few have caught the eye
> But head and shoulders above then all
> The late great C. B. Fry!

....

1971
My proudest *Wisden* possession is a 1971 that I found in a small bookshop in North Berwick. It didn't have a dust jacket and it wasn't in the best of condition, but I've added a replacement DJ and it looks just fine.

....

1932
The reason I regard my 1932 as my favourite is that I found a very small photograph of a young couple inside it. The back just says "mum and dad". Sometimes it saddens me that I don't know who they are, but most of the time I think it's wonderful that I now own a *Wisden* that someone in the past owned and treasured enough to put such a photograph inside.

....

2012
I had been going out with a girl from work for a couple of months and for my birthday in April she bought me the new *Wisden* (2012). I'd never been bought a *Wisden* by anyone, so I was pretty pleased. She packaged it nicely but left the receipt inside – "in case it's not the right thing".

She also told me that she had paid cash, so if I wanted to exchange it for something else she wouldn't mind. I didn't have the heart to tell her that I already had one which I'd bought for £27. But I thanked her so much and saw how happy she was at choosing me the right gift.

The next day I took it back to the high street shop and got a refund, put the one I had ordered on my bookshelf and didn't say a word. The following Saturday we were going out with friends to celebrate my birthday and she came around to my flat to pick me up. She spotted the book and to my astonishment lifted it off the shelf as I was sorting myself out, looking for my wallet and keys etc.

Later in the evening she asked me if I minded the message she had written in my *Wisden*. Crunch time! Did she know I had switched books? Had she spotted that the one on the shelf had no message inside? If I lied, would she start questioning me about everything else I had told her about myself? I was on a sticky wicket.

I told her the truth and waited. It transpired that she had written a very nice message on an early inside page and we both laughed when we realised that as her message was on the lines of "bowling a maiden over" any recipient would be happy to receive it.

....

1978

On my tenth birthday in 1978, I was surprised to unwrap a package containing a thick yellow book. Although I'd started to get keen on cricket, fuelled by Geoffrey Boycott's hundredth hundred and the early exploits of Ian Botham, I had no idea what *Wisden* was.

Looking at the battered volume on my bookcase today, it is hard to imagine that it was ever pristine, for I spent months poring over its every word. With the obsessive memory of a small boy, I learned statistics and scorecards that are still with me today, even though many of them are now rather out of date.

The birthday tradition continued, and still continues today. The older editions are looking rather careworn, and all have been well thumbed, but they take pride of place on a bookcase in the living room.

Then a couple of years ago I came across the 1976 and 1977 editions in an antiquarian bookshop in Cambridge and, on an impulse, bought them, although the 1976 was in an even worse state than some of my originals.

Not long afterwards, my sister bought me the 1964 and 1968 editions (to mark our respective years of birth) and I was hooked on collecting.

....

An interesting 1943 paperback

Have you ever wondered about the past history of your *Wisdens?* About the previous owner, or owners? What kind of person they were? Were they famous, or not famous? Was that *Wisden* taken to matches as a reference, or merely taken from a bookshelf occasionally? Was it the prized possession of a schoolboy who later became a Test player?

Many people feel that a signature or a dedication written in a *Wisden* diminishes its value. Since I have no intention of selling my *Wisdens,* I am honestly not worried, but I do feel that in some cases it can enhance a copy's value. Clearly if a *Wisden* were to be signed 'Ex libris W. G. Grace' and can be shown to be from WG's collection, that copy would have a value over and beyond its price simply as an old *Wisden.*

My 1943 *Wisden* is a case in point. It has a history. It was sent to Ion Calvocoressi by his mother for Christmas 1943 – and it is inscribed on the fly-leaf: 'ADC [Aide de Camp] to GOC [General Officer Commanding], Captain Ion Calvocoressi, MC, 30 Corps HQ, CMF [Central Mediterranean Force]' and stamped 'ADC 8th Army HQ'.

There is also a touching message from his mother, 'with love from Mummy, for Christmas 1943', with the family address in Belgravia. It is nice to remember that even war heroes have mothers!

Ion Calvocoressi was a genuine war hero and a person of considerable stature in postwar Britain – and a lifetime member of MCC. He won a Military Cross in the African Campaign in June 1942 while serving with 2 Battalion, Scots Guards. On June 13 Calvocoressi and his men were on a ridge at Bir Er Rigel (in Libya, about 25 miles SW of Tobruk) where they were attacked by two columns of the 21st Panzer division.

Unfortunately, two British armoured brigades had been moved away a few days before. The first attack was made on 17 Anti-tank Platoon under Lieutenant Calvocoressi's command. By the time the position was overrun, the platoon had knocked out five German tanks. Calvocoressi was captured, but escaped late the same night and walked 17 miles through the desert, rejoining his battalion the following morning. He was immediately awarded the MC.

The following month, Calvocoressi was wounded after rescuing the crew of a forward observation post which had come under enemy fire. In 1943, he became ADC to Lieutenant-General Sir Oliver Leese and served in North Africa, Italy (where in 1943, 30 Corps invaded Sicily on the left flank of the 8th Army) and Burma.

After the war Calvocoressi became a private-client stockbroker. He was High Sheriff of Kent in 1978-79. He was born in 1919 and died in 2007. By a nice coincidence, a boss of mine worked with Calvocoressi's son James at Hoare Govett during the 1980s.

....

Thank you, aunty

When I started to get interested in cricket as a teenager, particularly during the MCC tour of Australia in 1954/55, an aunty in England sent me a *Playfair Cricket Annual*, which I was thrilled to get, but she said the cricket book she had wanted to send she could not obtain. This turned out to be a *Wisden Cricketers' Almanack* which in due course I managed to buy to see what it was all about.

I vowed that when I was financially sound after I started work I would obtain *Wisden* each year. Finances had been particularly tight in our family, with my mother struggling to bring up six children on a limited budget, so cricket books of any description were not allowed.

When I did start work the majority of my meagre pay went to my mother for board. However, eventually my finances improved, and seeing an advert for Southern Booksellers and Publishing Co from the UK in a cricket magazine, I arranged for a copy of *Wisden* to be sent to me each year for many years, which I obtained earlier and at a lower cost than if I had waited until they appeared in the local bookshops in Perth.

Eventually I started to obtain back copies, with the majority obtained from Roger Page, the cricket book dealer in Victoria, and I was thrilled when I finally obtained my final back copy to have a full set in 1995.

....

1966

My boyfriend back in 1982 was a keen cricketer and after a local match he was having a good-humoured argument with one of the players from the other (winning) team. My boyfriend had been out LBW first ball and was quite adamant that he had nicked the ball first. He was losing the argument, as even the non-striker, one of his closest friends, said that his bat was a long way from his body.

In frustration and after a few pints, and with a certain tongue-in-cheek, he said that any man who had appeared in *Wisden* did not have need to cheat or lie. He had the floor, and when asked told us all that he was in the 1966 edition, 'almost' topping the batting averages for his school. The opposition player did not believe him, so one of the gathering telephoned home and asked his dad to check the *Wisden.* Sure enough, he was telling the truth.

The next day I bought a copy of *Wisden Cricket Monthly,* found a bookseller who sold *Wisdens,* and bought my boyfriend a 1966. I think that convinced him I was worth keeping. We were married two years later.

Each birthday and every Christmas I buy him *Wisdens*. He hasn't bought himself one for as long as I can remember, and on Christmas Day while others relax in front of the TV, he will immerse himself in his *Wisden*. As his collection now goes back into the nineteenth century and the books are noticeably thinner, he doesn't spend as long as he used to reading them.

....

1865
My best *Wisden* purchase was an 1865 original paperback edition. The truth is that my wife bought it for me from a jumble sale in Colchester back in 1973, so it wasn't really *my* 'best purchase'. She paid 50p for it and then hid it away for five months until Christmas Day.

....

1963
My husband has collected *Wisden* since before we met and his pride and joy is a 1963 hardback that his father bought him because they had been to the first day of the 1962 Lord's Test against Pakistan when 'their' idol, Fred Trueman, took six wickets including his 200th for England. My husband met his idol at a function some twenty years ago and took his 1963 in the hope of a signature: the great man did not let him down.

....

Splendid memories
As a youngster I fell in love with cricket when my father, a Hampshire supporter, first took me to see Gloucestershire play at Ashley Down in 1956, in which year I remember going to an experimental evening session against Yorkshire which finished at 8.30pm! The 1957 *Wisden* records that admission at 5.00pm attracted 1,200 supporters for a shilling.

I bought my first *Wisden* in 1962, the 1961 edition, which recorded Tom Graveney's decision to depart my county. Thereafter I bought the Almanack every year until 1973 when I got married.

One might have expected to have received the book as a present, but this never happened because its release in April did not coincide with my birthday or Christmas. There was no way I could wait to read about the previous season's events until the following cricket season was over and the news was 12 months old.

In 1973 I was asked by Mike Procter's agent to provide a statistical appendix to Mike's forthcoming book, *Cricket Buccaneer.* I had already given Mike a comprehensive set of his career statistics, all painstakingly produced on my portable typewriter.

His overseas performances were taken from several editions of the *South African Cricket Annual* which I had purchased from E. K. Brown of Cornwall. Mr Brown sent me leaflets with other books for sale which included back numbers of *Wisden.*

My wife Jenny and I were both working, with no children, and so I decided (with her permission) to start purchasing back numbers of *Wisden,* which I did from E. K. Brown and the other major stockist at the time, J. W. McKenzie, who is still in business today.

Throughout the 1970s I purchased secondhand editions back to 1947 which was the year of my birth. At the time I was a committee member of the Association of Cricket Statisticians and was Editor of their Quarterly Journal. I was quite envious of my fellow members Rob Brooke, Peter Wynne-Thomas and others who all had complete sets. There was no way I would be able to follow suit, given the expense and my material circumstances at the time, so I resolved that I would limit my collection to my living years.

Jenny bought me the 1946 edition as a surprise present, which was very expensive at the time – £15 I believe. In 1981 we started our family. With only one income and four young children to support, money was now tight but I had enough in the piggy bank to purchase each year's *Wisden.* In 2009 my children were grown up but still costing the Bank of Mum and Dad a fortune. However, I had spare cash courtesy of working abroad in my business as a construction consultant. I scrolled the internet and came across Wisdenworld. I was struck by its simple but friendly presentation.

I tried to purchase the 1864-78 facsimile set on line but the credit card did not work. The following morning I had a telephone call from the proprietor, Bill Furmedge. I duly completed the purchase and in so doing I was struck by Bill's enthusiasm. I could tell that his genuine passion for what he was doing superseded the fact that it was his business. Bill told me that his original intention was the same as mine – to collect the *Wisdens* from his birth date – but he had gone on to complete his set. We spoke on the phone a few times and I realised that with guidance from Bill and a financial business plan, I could collect a full set which would be mainly affordable Willows reprints.

Over the next twelve months I purchased all but five of the *Wisdens* I needed from Wisdenworld. The remaining five were in the course of being printed by Willows and in July 2012 I purchased the 1939 Almanack. My collection was complete. It had taken 50 years. My inspiration to achieve this goal was Bill Furmedge and Wisdenworld.

Gentlemen versus Players
Pitching Amateur 'gainst Pro
An archaic system from Empire Days
By '62 it had to go!

....

1917

My grandfather is in *Wisden!* That's why I began collecting. He topped the batting averages for his school and he is in the 1917 edition. Even though I now have a full set, it is the pride I feel when I see his name on page 321 within the Public School Averages that makes that edition so special

I bought my 1917 from a dealer in London for £45 in 1975. I wasn't sure whether it was a bargain, a good price or whether I was being taken advantage of – it didn't matter. I had saved enough to buy it and it was a piece of my life, my family's history that I wanted to have.

....

1982

My husband was impossible to buy gifts for. He has never been the trendiest of men, nor has he been particularly into music, so gifts were mostly aftershave, DVDs (usually sport related) or DIY tools. When our youngest daughter was eight she got into the habit of taking a cup of tea into the spare room where he used to watch Sky Sports, and one evening she came back downstairs telling me she had a really good idea for his birthday.

"Another one of those yellow books," she said.

Now, if the truth be told, I actually thought he read the same book over and over again, and I told my daughter this: I had no idea they were different. She then told me that they had years on the side and she had seen him reading a 1981.

When I got home the following day my daughter and I went into the spare room, and low and behold, he had six of these yellow books: all had different years on the side, 1976 through to 1981. A little while later we went into W. H. Smith and saw that they had the 1982. I knew he didn't have it, so I bought it.

Since then I have always bought him the new almanack each year, along with the odd one going backwards, and now he is complete until 1957.

I don't 'get' *Wisden,* but I am happy in the knowledge that he is not alone. We bought him a subscription to the Wisden Collectors' Club, and even though I don't read the stuff that comes through, I know he likes to feel that he is not alone in not being trendy and loving yellow books about cricket.

Disgraceful scenes in Melbourne
With that Chappell brothers pact
To bowl the last ball underarm
The all-time cowards' act!

The (lack of) luck of the Irish

My story on how I started my *Wisden* collection is a sentimental one. I received a phone call at work from my wife Maureen one day with some news of great importance.

While talking to an Irish business client, the lady in question asked Maureen if she knew anybody who was interested in cricket. My wife told the lady: "My husband and son love the game." The lady then said that her uncle had died in England and had left some cricket books in his estate to her and her brother, both of whom knew nothing of the game.

The cricket books included a set of *Wisdens* from 1958-2005. "Unbelievable" was my reply, quickly adding: "I will pick them up tomorrow." Unfortunately tomorrow never came and they were sold as part of the estate.

When I later recounted to my mum the story of the *Wisdens,* she told me that her father (my granddad) had a couple of books, and she was sure they were somewhere in the loft. Sure enough, she soon found two *Wisdens,* 1962 and 1963 – the years my two brothers were born.

Mum said that she was sure they were meant for them. The edition for my birth year was not there, and so she said that she would start a collection for me. Starting in 1979, the year I was married, she brought me four books.

Sadly, two years later mum died. I am still collecting *Wisdens* and still get a thrill when I add a book to the collection, and I still thank my mum and the Irish client for starting me on my way.

....

1970

Not long after I started collecting – 1970 was the first *Wisden* someone bought for me when I was 12 – my mum Gillian spotted a 1968 hardback (good condition plus dust jacket) in a junk shop at the bottom of Sutton High Street.

This was probably about 1973 or 1974. She went inside and fiddled around with a few things, the way you do, before pretending to spot the *Wisden.* She asked the owner how much it was. He looked at it and said: "Nice book" (which it was) and then spotted the date. "Oh, it's an old one," he said. "You can have it for 50p." I've still got it.

On the other side of the coin, a few years later I had a problem with the washbasin in my bedroom. At the time my *Wisdens* were shelved nearby. The plumber who came to mend the tap spotted them.

"Ah, they're cricket books, aren't they? I was fixing something for an elderly lady recently, and she had lots of those. She didn't know what to do with them.

In the end she burned them." Seeing my horrified expression, he tried to cheer me up: "Don't worry, hers were old ones, really old. Not nice new ones like yours." He didn't quite understand why I felt even worse after that.

....

A quite wonderful gesture

While working as a newspaper reporter in Sussex during the 1970s I was lucky to meet up with a local councillor who shared my passion for cricket. He also loved cricket books and was an avid *Wisden* collector. It was him who started me off by giving me some spare softbacks from the 1950s.

He had become an MCC member in 1924 and after buying his yearly almanack direct from *Wisden* was surprised to learn that from 1949 his membership of the MCC qualified him for a free hardback edition.*

Apparently he had watched the Lord's and the Oval Tests against Australia in the glorious summer of 1948 and been present when the tourists hit 721 in a day against Essex at Southend. Like most cricket lovers around the world he was besotted with Bradman and expressed genuine sorrow that he had failed in his last Test innings, thereby not achieving the Test career average of 100.

As a memento of the Australian score against Essex, this chap had put together a scrapbook with newspaper reports and the scorecard that he had picked up at the game and filled in by taking the information from the newspaper a day or so later. A number of England signatures were gathered during the season, and after the Australians left for home his father suggested that he write to Lord's to find out if they had the contact details of anyone in Australia who might be able to put him in touch with any of the Australian players or officials.

Within a couple of weeks he received a reply from Colonel Kerr at the MCC who gave him the contact details of the secretary of the Australian Cricket Board, and he duly wrote a letter. Six months later a sturdy envelope arrived and within was one of the most amazing notes.

His original letter to Australia had found its way to Don Bradman who had personally written to his teammates from the Oval Test of 1948 and asked them to put their signature on the back of a photograph of the Eleven. On the back of the photograph my friend counted ten signatures and the accompanying note on headed notepaper read: "Sorry I could not get all eleven, but Johnston now lives as far from me as Moscow is to London and it proved difficult" – signed Don Bradman.

To gather, post and organise a photograph to be signed by a group of players is noteworthy enough, but to do it across Australia and at the bequest of a young man from England speaks more than anything I can bring to mind of the generous nature of probably the greatest batsmen to have lived.

There was a smaller envelope within the package that contained my friend's original letter to the MCC, with a note at the foot, intended for the recipient in Australia: "I believe you will hear from the above gentleman in due course; any assistance you can offer would be appreciated, RK." So the Secretary of the MCC, Colonel Rait Kerr, had also tried to help further by forwarding the original letter.

> Worrell, Walcott, Weekes, Wes Hall
> Marshall, Griffiths, Sobers, Haines
> There's something magic in that Bajan sun
> Where so much talent lives and reigns!

*It has been suggested that MCC members of 25 years standing used to receive a 'complimentary' almanack from Wisden for each subsequent year of their membership. It is not known whether part of the MCC annual subscription paid for this, but this seems likely as in 1914 the MCC subscription rose by 9%, which caused some uproar. It seems that these copies may not have been included in any print run information and it has been suggested that the first complimentary copies were sent out in 1914, primarily to former Public School cricketers (officers) serving in the Great War. It was deemed a patriotic gesture and the complimentary copies continued being sent to others until 1963. If this is true it does throw into question the 'assumed' print runs of the WW2 editions, but then again it could be a wonderful myth.

....

Love conquers all, even a Wisden collection
Why do I buy my husband *Wisdens?*

I only found out that he liked them by accident. His best friend from his university days contacted him after a gap of 24 years and he eventually came up for a weekend.

Their conversation eventually got on to cricket. Did they still play? Did they go to matches? His friend asked him, did he still collect *Wisdens?* My husband said "no" and that he had to sell the ones he had a few years ago. I never knew he had owned any or that he had sold them, so a few days after his friend had left I asked him about them.

Matter-of-factly he told me that he had sold them to raise the money for my 40th birthday trip to Venice. He had lost his job a couple of months before my birthday but he was adamant that none of the plans he had made would be changed. I found out where we were going when we arrived at London Victoria.

He told me how much he had got for his *Wisdens* and then he told me how rare some of them were, and despite it being six years ago and our circumstances were now much better, I felt awful that a set of books he had spent 30-plus years collecting, along with many his father had given him, had been sold.

Since then, I have made a point of buying him *Wisdens* whenever I can. The first one I bought him was a 1934: my knowledge on *Wisden* isn't that bad now, and I do know that every collector should have a '34.

> That golden summer of '47
> Denis Compton – what a joy
> A masterclass in batting skill
> From the pin-up 'Brylcreem Boy'!

....

1978

On my tenth birthday in 1978, I was surprised to unwrap a package containing a thick yellow book. Although I'd started to get keen on cricket, fuelled by Geoffrey Boycott's hundredth hundred and the early exploits of Ian Botham, I had no idea what *Wisden* was.

Looking at the battered volume on my bookcase today, it is hard to imagine that it was ever pristine, for I spent months poring over its every word. With the obsessive memory of a small boy I learned statistics and scorecards that are still with me today, even though many of them are now rather out of date.

The birthday tradition continued, and still continues today. The older editions are looking rather careworn, and all have been well thumbed, but they take pride of place on a bookcase in the living room.

Then a couple of years ago I came across the 1976 and 1977 editions in an antiquarian bookshop in Cambridge and, on an impulse, bought them, although the 1976 was in an even worse state than some of my originals. Not long afterwards, my sister bought me the 1964 and 1968 editions (to mark our respective years of birth) and I was hooked on collecting.

....

What kind of collection do you want
For some, the goal of a *Wisden* collection is the acquisition of a set that is both uniform and pristine. Undoubtedly there is much to recommend the handsome appearance of such a set, which undeniably adorns a bookcase.

For me, however, there is a separate charm in each volume being slightly different, so that each year has its own feel and character, and for this reason I rather like the different coloured lettering of the hardbacks between 1965 and 1978, and have never considered purchasing the replacement dust wrappers. I may perhaps be making a virtue of necessity, since a perfect set has always been well beyond my means and some of my *Wisdens* are far from pristine, but as I will explain, this has been part of the fun of collecting.

Acquiring a set of *Wisden* has taken me from boyhood into middle age, and some volumes in the collection feel almost like signposts on the road of my life. Thus, for example, the 1916 Willows reprint arrived on the day I broke off an engagement, so my perception of the obituaries of Grace and Trumper is forever associated with the turbulent emotions of that period of my life. By contrast, my 1908 edition, which is an original, is a somewhat quirky copy, having been rebound many years ago in a curious purple cloth, now rather the worse for wear. It would be sniffed at by the purist collector, yet it is one of my most treasured volumes.

This is not only because it records what A. A. Thomson would later describe as 'The Googly Summer' when the South African touring side included as many as four leg-break and googly bowlers in its line-up, but also because the day I received it was also the day in 1993 when I opened my front door to meet a girl who only a few months later would become my wife.

Coming up to date, the 1937 Willows reprint that completed my collection in December 2011 arrived within a few days of the birth of our sixth child. Most of my *Wisdens* between 1906 and 1936 are rebound originals – many of them what one dealer terms 'defective', that is, they lack the photo plate or a few pages – in an array of different bindings, including red cloth (1906), yellow cloth (1923) and black cloth (1906, 1911, 1914) as well as the more conventional brown. They would probably be of little value to a collector. One, however, is an almost pristine, softback 1930 edition which one might expect to command a high price. I acquired it at a knock-down price, however, because unlike the others, which have lost pages along the way through constant handling, it was wrongly printed and lacks one section, while another is duplicated.

This seems to be a recurring problem with *Wisden:* I have seen much the same in 1924 and 1974 editions. It would be interesting to know how many such faulty copies are still in circulation. Whatever the answer, I am pleased to have this 1930 edition in my collection, as it gives a feel for what it might have been like to handle a softback *Wisden* eighty years ago.

My postwar *Wisdens* are similarly something of a mixed bunch, some yellow, some brown, and were collected more or less at random as I came across them. Some were Christmas presents, others picked up secondhand, and two even purchased from Sporting Handbooks following a letter in *The Cricketer* indicating that a few old volumes were still available from the original publishers. Thus my 1959 edition is still in almost pristine condition, although it did suffer slightly from being in my rucksack during a thunderstorm some years ago.

My first *Wisden* in 1978 also happened to be the last to be published by Sporting Handbooks. Since then, there has been a greater tendency to uniformity, and many of the volumes in the 1980s and 1990s feel very similar. Perhaps the introduction of the photograph on the front cover in 2003 has something to recommend it, for this reason if for no other!

....

Why does my husband read Wisden?
Because with two growing daughters he realised pretty early on that he would need to read something while he waited in the bathroom queue.

"Now they can wait!"

....

2000

The collecting of The Yellow Bible began for me in 2000. For most of my life I've enjoyed watching and listening to cricket, but never been in a financial position to buy the book. The 2000 copy was a Father's Day present from my sons, so in a way you could blame them for my obsession!

My first thought was to continue to buy all the years after 2000, but then trips to Cambridge and Hay-on-Wye changed that. The books for the '80s and '90s weren't that expensive, so that was the first alteration to my collection.

We had a holiday booked to Cornwall in 2001. My collection was missing a few copies from the '80s and '90s, so I made a list of book shops in the area we were going to visit – the obsession taking over now! My sons, aged nine and eight, joined in too. Every bookshop we visited they would be looking for the yellow book. Having purchased my missing copies, the '70s seemed not too expensive to buy.

After seeing a copy of 1978 with no dust jacket in one shop in the morning, I decided not to buy it. Then during the day while doing family stuff I wondered, will I see that book again? So, near to closing time, my wife said stay here with the boys and off she ran … only to return twenty minutes later with the 1978. So the second alteration was to collect back to my birth year of 1967.

The next collecting phase was quite slow. After going to antique and book fairs, I picked up various '70s and '60s editions. Yes, I had moved the goalposts again to start my collection at 1960. I also decided to collect hardbacks back to 1974 and the softbacks to 1960.

I saw an advert in a cricket magazine for replacement dust jackets for the 1970s, so my 1978 wouldn't look out of place with my other books. So now the collection was growing!

Then came the internet age, appearing in our household for the first time in 2004. With access to AbeBooks and eBay, the goalposts moved again: this time the collection was to start at 1946. So the collection was growing, but where to put them all?

Bookcase space was very limited so the books had to be doubled up, but not forever. Then in 2008 I did a web search for Wisden and came across Wisdenworld.com. They had my missing early 1970s. So now I had a great source of *Wisdens* and a dealer who was honest about the books he was selling. I was browsing many websites and book fairs and would pick up books now and then. With my collection nearly complete from 1946 onwards, I was wishing that I could afford the prewar editions.

After many chats with Wisdenworld it was recommended that I check out the Willows reprints. Well, that was it – the collection would start from 1864. As of now I only need 13 to complete the quest from the 1920s and 1930s. The first fifteen were brought in 2012 (Lowe & Brydone reprints) thanks to a bonus from my employer.

Having moved house, the collection is now on the bookcases. It's a marvellous sight, starting with 1864 to 1878 pink, 1879 to 1945 tan and brown covers, then from 1946 yellow softbacks and 1974 to present yellow dust jacketed hardbacks.

The first thing I read when obtaining a book are the Notes by the Editor. It gives you an insight into what was happening at that time and of course his point of view. You may agree or disagree, but *Wisden* will still hold all the cricket information that one needs. I know that in the internet age the information is all online, but where is the fun in that? Just pick up a year of *Wisden* and thumb through what you need, then get side-tracked and read about something else in that year and forget why you picked it up in the first place.

It's all about holding history in your hand and feeling part of it.

So I say, thank you John Wisden for a most glorious book and a big thank you also to my family for putting up with this Yellow Book obsession.

....

1886

Finding my 1886 was a stroke of luck. I was at a conference on employee benefits in Harrogate in 2002. India were thrashing England at Headingley and I was keen to get the updated score. Casually mentioning to the chap in front of me in the lunch queue that I'd rather be at the cricket, he instantly agreed. I then said something about having to read all about India's exploits in the next day's papers, to which he replied, better still in next year's *Wisden.*

I had found a kindred spirit and before long we were chatting about all things *Wisden.* My collection was back to 1893, he was lacking the first two. We exchanged cards and I emailed him when I returned to London to bemoan England's poor showing in the Test match. He replied, and after an entertaining email exchange asked if I would be interested in buying his spare 1886. Naturally I was. He said that if I bought him lunch the next time he was in London, I could have it. I think the lunch cost me £120! We now meet at least three or four times a year and I think the next lunch is on him.

....

Almost a full set in one

I was learning the ropes at the *Melbourne Age,* from sport to police rounds to finance. One of the feature stories my finance editor liked was a story about the value of collecting *Wisden* and how they were a hedge against inflation, and for the cricket lover, superannuation at its most pleasurable. The business editor of the paper, Barry Flint, read the story and approached me one day and said his neighbour had a pristine run of *Wisden* from the 1890s and would I be interested in them? The lady's husband had died and she needed to downsize. Was I interested!

They were all in near mint condition, all limps or paper covers, about 80 of them. I paid a fair price – thanks to my cricket-loving dad who advanced the money – and suddenly I had a meaningful run of the wonderful English cricketing bible. So proud was I that I made protective yellow cardboard jackets for them all and carefully Letrasetted the year on to each of them uniformly. It was the greatest of finds. I just happened to be in the right place at the right time, and my *Wisden* set, now stretching back to volume one, remains a pride and joy cornerstone of almost 50 years of collecting.

Ken Piesse *(www.cricketbooks.com.au)* is the author of 66 books, the majority on cricket, including his most recent *Encyclopaedia of Australian Cricket Players*

> From an obituary in the 'Sporting Times'
> Was born the ultimate of clashes
> The greatest contest in the World
> Known simply as 'The Ashes'!

....

1965

My mother used to buy me a *Wisden* every year. The first one I received was the 1962. When she gave me my 1965 I didn't like the fact that it looked out of place, so I threw away the yellow dust jacket. I did that with every one until 1980.

I bought my first *Wisden* from a friend at school in 1983. He charged me 50p for a 1972 linen cloth edition. Even though it was in awful condition I read it from cover to cover. I replaced it a few years ago. I still have it, but if I looked at it once more, the chances are it would fall apart.

I played for a village team in one of the Yorkshire leagues; it is sensible if I don't mention which one. They were given a job lot of cricket items by the widow of a former chairman and amongst them were twenty or so *Wisdens,* one being a 1917 paperback. They sat in the clubhouse untouched for weeks until one of the committee members saw me reading the 1917. I was asked if I would like it and I said yes. It could be mine for a fair donation to the club's coffers, he said, which I duly made.

> The old boys at the MCC
> Were moaning at each other
> About their *Wisden* 1965
> And that new-fangled yellow cover!

....

Not so much a Brief Encounter of the Wisden kind

From 1959 through to 1975, I was one of those chaps who wore a bowler and always carried an umbrella on the commuter train from South Croydon into London, and it is another hat-wearing umbrella-carrying fellow traveller that I have to thank for getting me into *Wisden.*

Sitting in our carriage, this strange soul would read what looked like the same book every day. One morning he caught my eye as I peered over my newspaper. We struck up a conversation and I asked him what was he reading.

"*Wisden* 1957," he said. "Laker's nineteen-for." I was quite interested in cricket and each summer I spent a few days watching Surrey at The Oval and in 1955 I had seen England play South Africa.

My train companion and I chatted for the rest of the journey and I mentioned that I had seen Peter May score a hundred against South Africa at The Oval in '55. The next day my friend sat across from me on the train and gave me a 1956 *Wisden* with a paper bookmark on the page of the aforementioned Test.

I read the report, digested the scorecards and then flicked back to the beginning of the SA tour and read through the reports and scorecards. Before I knew it we had arrived in London. I apologised and he just smiled. As I went to give him back his 1956, he said: "It's yours – I have three copies."

Then he asked me if I noticed something about the Test match at The Oval. I must have looked a little bemused and he said: "May didn't score a hundred."

Over the coming years my good friend and I chatted a lot about cricket and he attended my wedding in 1964 along with his wife. After we had retired we spent a few afternoons at The Oval, but we actually preferred to watch local cricket and it was during one of those afternoons that, for me, he summed up *Wisden* collecting when he referred back to my "belief" that May had scored a hundred.

"*Wisden* reminds us of matches, of players, of catches; it takes us back to the season, the game, the day, even the session or a particular over, and in most cases it gently reminds us that we might have seen things through rose-coloured spectacles." For me it summed up why I read *Wisden,* and although I never caught up with my friend in terms of the number of *Wisdens* we both owned, when he passed away in 2008 his wife kindly gave me many I did not have.

1978 is a popular Wisden
Many of us probably received our first *Wisden* in childhood as a Christmas or birthday present, and I am no exception. I was presented with the 1978 edition by a benevolent uncle on the eve of that year's Benson & Hedges Cup Final, which was also my first visit to Lord's.

Although my birthday is in January, my uncle felt I would obtain more enjoyment from the *Wisden* in the summer, and his judgment proved sound. That *Wisden* went everywhere with me that summer – there are still grains of sand from a Welsh beach stuck in the spine – and I was already hooked. Yet at that stage I had little thought of building up a collection. That possibility only started to present itself to me when my parents gave me the 1977 edition for Christmas that year, having picked it up cheaply in a local secondhand bookshop.

Initially my plans were simply to collect *Wisdens* from the 1970s: that seemed a neat cut-off, and in those days I was primarily interested in the performances of the players of my own era. The discovery of a well-worn 1958 hardback in my school library when I went to secondary school in September 1979 scotched that idea.

I was fascinated by the 1957 season: England's demolition of West Indies was a pleasing antidote to the emerging dominance of Clive Lloyd's side in my own period, while the county championship of 28 matches per side, the sole county competition, utterly dominated by Surrey, was something of a revelation to a boy used to a much-reduced competition vying for attention with three limited over tournaments. To this day 1957 is one of my favourite seasons.

My parents, recognising my burgeoning interest, gave me two *Wisdens* from the 1960s for Christmas in 1979, and my parameters shifted to embrace postwar issues. So when in 1981 I came across a run of hardback *Wisdens* in a bookshop in Bournemouth, beginning with the 1939 edition, for £5 each, my plan was to purchase the 1939 edition and sell it on, to fund the purchase of as many of the others as I (or my parents) could afford. Needless to say, that 1939 hardback is still in my collection, as are several others from that run, my only regret being that I could not afford to buy them all. Even so, it was some years before I was able to reimburse my indulgent parents for the outlay they had made on the purchase.

Through the 1980s my collection grew slowly, with the addition of a few rather tatty issues from the 1950s from a bookshop in Hay-on-Wye, and several more from various bookshops in Oxford while I was a student. As time wore on, I began to realise that collecting *Wisden* was a potentially expensive hobby, and that it would take me a very long time to build up a decent collection if I relied on fortuitous discoveries of cheap copies.

In 1989, when I began my career as a civil servant, I found myself in the unexpected position of earning a reasonable income and having, as a single man with no commitments, some disposable income.

That summer I read a book review – possibly in the ACS Journal – about the 1887 Willows reprint, on the strength of which I decided to try it out. The result was almost like receiving my first *Wisden* eleven years earlier – and indeed the 1887 edition is in many ways so different from the 1978 that it was like starting a new collection. I immediately contacted Willows and bought up the back issues of their reprints, and so started to build up my collection from the other end of the *Wisden* spectrum. Willows reprints now form a substantial part of my collection – all as the result of a single book review.

Some years later I received a catalogue from a dealer; I cannot now remember how I came to be on his mailing list. He was offering a copy of the 1909 *Wisden* for £55 – not exactly cheap, but less expensive than others I had come across, and as I had recently been promoted and was still single, I felt I could afford to splash out. I continued to do so for several months, until at the end of that year I met the lady who was to become my wife, and my priorities changed somewhat.

There followed something of a hiatus, as marriage and then children took my attention, but in 1998 an advertisement in *Wisden Cricket Monthly* caught my eye, stating that a dealer would be at a book fair in Haywards Heath, where I was then living, later that month. He sold me a relatively inexpensive 1925 edition – part of the book was misbound, which reduced the price slightly – and added me to his mailing list.

A few months later he sent me a catalogue listing a cheap 1913 edition. When I rang to purchase it, he candidly described it as "an utterly ghastly copy" (a view I don't share), and told me that he had some others in similar condition that he would bring to the next book fair. He was true to his word, and in this way I began to fill in the substantial gaps in my collection, purchasing 'defective' *Wisdens* at a price that I could afford and justify alongside the expense of raising a large family.

The process has still been slow, but in December 2012 the Willows reprint of the 1937 edition completed my collection, some 33 years after that first edition.

With my collection now complete, are my days of *Wisden* purchasing now at an end? Perhaps not. The *Wisden* bug is a strong one, and although there are no longer any gaps to fill, there are some rather tatty-looking softbacks that could do with upgrading to hardbacks. And then there are the reprints. I love these, and they are in far better condition than any original. But sometimes I feel that an original has more appeal to it – the sense of age, and the knowledge that it has passed through other hands and been on bookcases in homes far different from my own. I would not replace my reprints, but if I could afford it, I would consider purchasing originals to go alongside them. So it seems that a *Wisden* collection is never really complete – merely at a different stage of transition!

....

1979

My first *Wisden* was a 1979, bought in Debenhams in Plymouth in 1981 by my mum after she reluctantly told me (probably to keep me quiet) that she'd get me one if I could find one ... and unbelievably in the bargains section there was the previous year's. Since then it has become a traditional birthday present. My dad used to pick up the odd older one if he came across any at antiques fairs, but it was only really in the last ten years that I started properly collecting and filling the gaps. Most infill has come via eBay, bookshops, and family who have picked them up from dealers.

It's fair to say that eBay can be a bit hit and miss. This has slowed somewhat since coming to Oz, although I did pick up 1938 and 1939 on ebay.com.au for much cheaper prices than I would ever have got in the UK. I guess there are fewer collectors out here.

I also won a signed large print format *Wisden* last year on a *Wisden* twitter comp, and then 'did the double', winning a *Wisden on Yorkshire* book too. Add to the almanacks the anthologies, a pretty much complete set of *Playfairs,* nearly every issue of the *Wisden Books of Cricket Records and Test Cricket,* and plenty of stats books, and it's not a bad set. My dad started with the Willows reprints when they started, and he has the complete *Pelhams* (what was the B&H/C&G) *Cricket Yearbook* run.

Between us, we've a decent set.

....

My stag weekend

This is not a story of wild drinking and being dumped on the Yorkshire Moors with only a 50p piece and the werewolves for company – that came later.

My best man and I have been friends for 21 years: we met when we both started secondary school and we even ended up at the same university. At uni, we played rugby in the winter and cricket until the year ended around the middle of June. His sport is rugby and mine is cricket.

I have collected Wisdens off and on for about ten years. I don't have many – 22 – but as I get older hopefully I will expand the collection. He even bought me the 2006 for my birthday! He was the obvious choice to be my best man when I got married in 2008 and I was more than happy to leave my stag weekend –

who has a stag night these days? – in his capable hands.

He picked me up at 8am on Friday, July 4, from my flat in York in a minibus containing six of my friends and with him driving. We then picked up two more mates at a service station where we also had a good breakfast. When we finished breakfast he gave us all a large brown envelope: inside was a yellow Wisden dust jacket – the older traditional style. At the top it read:

Paul Ferguson's Stag Weekend

Then below:

WISDEN AWFUL CRICKETERS' TOUR JULY 2008

There followed the woodcut image and below that was the itinerary of the stag weekend, starting with a trip to the FP semi-final at Chester-le-Street that very day, then a journey to a hotel in Durham and finally a flight the next morning to Prague. All of which was itemised in the old Wisden style on the dust jacket, along with various other little challenges and dares, which I won't go into.

On the inside flap of the dust jacket was a photograph of me and a brief potted history of me and my future wife; on the inside back cover flap was a list of all the rugby and cricket matches my best man and I had seen together (the print was small) and on the back cover a list of every Wisden I owned, with a particular family memory alongside it from the year. He had put the whole thing together and it looked fantastic.

I still have the yellow jacket: it is torn and faded, but then most are!

....

1916

I realised fairly early on in my *Wisden* collecting days that a 1916 was going to be expensive. When I retired in 1995 after working for the same company for 38 years, my leaving gift was a rather lovely 1916 paperback. I was amazed that almost everyone at the law firm where I worked had signed the card to accompany the *Wisden,* and more surprised and deeply moved that they had collected enough to merit such a gift.

....

1912: An inspiring inscription

I already had a hardback 1912 *Wisden* but it was the inscription in the catalogued volume that caught my eye: "Wishing Daddy a very happy birthday, and many happy returns of the day from Niel. July 5th 1912."

Then in other handwriting were the Latin words: "Dulce et decorum est pro patria mori. Finis coronat opus. 20 July 1916." ("How sweet and fitting it is to die for one's country. The end crowns the work.")

It seemed that the son who gave the book to his father in 1912 died on July 20, 1916. I tried to decipher pencil notes alongside the Latin words that referred to pages carrying reports of Rugby School matches and averages. The Rugby School side v Marlborough in 1911 was:

R. A. Boddington
J. L. Andrews
I. F. L. Elliot
A. de Selincourt
G. G. Jackson
J. T. Bretherton
T. P. Norris
F. W. Watson
N. W Wadham
B. W. Fagan
R. M. Aston

But I could find no connections with a 'Niel'. However, I had become so intrigued by the mystery that I felt compelled to buy the book, and eventually I was successful in the auction and the book arrived.

Once it was in my hands, I discovered someone who might be able to help me in my research. There is a superb website named the Great War Forum and one member, in America, has many of the school rolls of honour and is willing to answer requests for information.

I sent him the names of the eleven who played for Rugby School against Marlborough in 1911. This was the message I received back from Dick Flory: "I must say that this mystified me initially because while they were all educated at Rugby School, the only man on your list who died during the war was Ronald Moseley Aston* and he died on March 14, 1915. So I then checked my Rugby School Register for brothers of the men on the list and found your man, who is not on the list you sent but rather is the brother of Brian Walter Fagan, who is on your list.

"Niel is 2nd Lieut Niel Fagan, 6th Bn, The Rifle Brigade, the younger brother of Brian Walter Fagan. Niel was born on February 26, 1896, the son of Sir Patrick James Fagan, KCIE, CSI the Financial Commissioner of the Punjab and his wife, Emily Francis. He was educated at Rugby School from 1909 to 1911 where he played cricket, and at Pembroke College, Cambridge. He was commissioned in the 6th Bn in November 1914 and went to France on July 5th 1915 where he served as the Bombing Officer of the 1st Bn, The Rifle Brigade.

"On the Somme on July 1, 1916, he led the two centre platoons in the attack at Thiepval and while attending to injured men in the open he was severely wounded in three places and lay in no man's land wounded for 48 hours. He died of his wounds at Chichester on July 20, 1916, at the age of 20."

Dick Flory gave the sources as *Memorials of Rugbeians Who Fell in the Great War, Volume III,* and *Rugby School Register, Annotated, 1892-1921.*

So, I had discovered the identity of Niel. The proud schoolboy had given his father the *Wisden* that recorded the cricketing achievements of his older brother Brian for Rugby School in 1911. According to *Wisden,* B. W. Fagan "bowled extremely well" for Rugby against Marlborough in 1911 when he topped the school's bowling averages.

Four years after giving that *Wisden* to his "Daddy", Niel was mortally wounded on the first day of the Somme.

A couple of weeks after my discovery in June 2010, I set out for a day's cricket at Arundel with Mike Spurrier, an expert on cricket and the military, who wrote a series of articles on 'Cricketers Brave' in *Wisden Cricket Monthly.* On the way, we made a detour to visit the cemetery in Chichester where Niel is buried. We soon found the elegant memorial on which the names of 89 war dead are listed; Niel Fagan's grave is next to it. I placed the 1912 *Wisden* on the memorial and on Niel's grave.

Niel was clearly having a greater effect on me that I could ever have imagined. I then discovered via AbeBooks that there was a portrait of Niel in a bookshop in York. It arrived with a brief biography on the reverse, taken from the *Rugby School Register.*

The next turn of events was extraordinary. I saw a 1902 hardback *Wisden* listed in a catalogue. The listing mentioned a 'defect': a new owner had inscribed his name, and crossed out the previous owner's name – something I had never seen before. But despite the crossing out with two lines, I felt I recognised the 'N' and saw the possibility that the surname could be Fagan.

The dealer had a close look and was unsure, so he generously offered to send me the book on approval. When it arrived, I inspected the signature with a magnifying glass and compared the writing with the inscription "from Niel" in the 1912 *Wisden*. There was no doubt: the 1902 *Wisden* once belonged to Niel Fagan.

Niel was aged six in 1902, but we can understand the pleasure he must have had in giving the 1912 *Wisden* to his father ten years later, so it is quite likely the teenage schoolboy would then have collected other *Wisdens*. Perhaps Niel set out to collect *Wisdens* going back to his birth date of 1896.

Gaining further inspiration by handling a *Wisden* owned by Niel, I did more detective work to trace a relative. A search led me to America and an email address for a relative of Niel who I thought must be aged around 90. I sent him the outline of the Niel Fagan saga.

Fortunately, he is much younger, and he responded within an hour to say: "You got the right person!"

Niel's elder brother, Brian Walter Fagan, the schoolboy bowler named in the 1912 *Wisden,* has a surviving adopted son, also Brian, who from 1967 to 2003 was Professor of Anthropology at the University of California, Santa Barbara.

Professor Fagan wrote: "How nice of you to write about Niel Fagan, who was, of course, my late father's brother. You have told me more about him than I ever knew before, as my father never spoke about him, or about the war for that matter. He lost a leg on the Somme."

After providing more family details, he ended: "It means a lot to me that you got in touch and I appreciate it. Any further information you would care to pass on would be valued. You've made our day." It rather made my day too!

After further correspondence, we came across a further coincidence involving the Cambridge college where Niel's nephew was educated. Professor Fagan also went to Rugby School – as was the family tradition – but he did not know he had followed in his uncle's footsteps when he too went to Pembroke College to study archaeology and anthropology: "My parents never told me that Niel went there!"

He said: "I think my father erased all memories of the war from his mind. All I knew about Niel was the inscription in the Rugby chapel." Niel's name is listed there among the many Old Rugbeians who perished, with the exhortation: "Let those who come after see to it that their name be not forgotten."

Niel's name has certainly not been forgotten: I told the saga of *Wisden's* 'unknown soldier' in the 2012 *Wisden* and Robert Winder retold the story at the end of *The Little Wonder.*

Niel inspired me to embark on another project – updating the Roll of Honour of the cohorts of cricketers whose obituaries appeared in the *Wisdens* of the First World War. The result of my researches will be seen in *Wisden on the Great War* to be published in April 2014.

[*Lt Ronald Aston's obituary appears in the 1916 *Wisden* immediately below that of his father, Capt Frederick Aston. Both were killed in action in 1915.]

Andrew Renshaw

....

Is there snobbery in Wisden collecting?
Buying and having *Wisdens* is an immense enjoyment for me. Lawrence Booth said that *Wisden* was a social history and if you read through the pages over the years you would get a sense of the country and its politics. I couldn't agree more, but recently I have come across snobbery in collecting. I used to believe that some sellers were simply treating *Wisdens* as a business and I fully support the argument that *Wisdens* are indeed a business, but recently, and maybe it is me, I have come across a certain snobbery.

While attending an auction in 2012 I began chatting to someone who I later found out to be a *Wisden* dealer. Rather than naming names, which would be discourteous in the least, I will just say that it was not anyone to do with the Wisden Collectors' Club; indeed if it was, I am certain that I would never have become a member.

I bid on and won a rebind from the 1920s, as the catalogue stated, "lacking original covers". I was quite pleased with myself and I proudly boasted to the gentleman alongside me that I had completed my collection back to 1920. His response confused me a little: "So will you be carrying on or just upgrading the poor ones you have?" While I pondered my response he chipped in with: "A collection of originals is what counts, anything else seems pointless." "Pointless!" – the jumped-up little oik!

My wife has accompanied me on many a stroll through the back streets and small towns of England indulging my craving for *Wisden.* She has witnessed first-hand the look of pure joy when a missing edition has been found, especially in Newport around ten years ago when I spotted a rebound 1937 (lacking covers) for £2. But to my shame, ever since that dealer's words hit my ears, I have regretted not coming back with something more than "Oh" which sort of trickled out of my mouth in embarrassment.

His comments got me thinking, and when I look back at the times when I have bought from the established dealer community I do recall instances when I enquired about a 1930s or 1940s edition and heard a distinct change in attitude when I mentioned it was a rebound edition I was after.

Now, maybe I have been spoilt in my relationships with some people, but I also tend to find some sellers abrupt. On a couple of occasions when seeking rebinds for specific years I have been politely informed that rebinds are ten to the dozen, and I have been told to keep ringing and the ones I want are certain to come in. The people I buy from now are those who contact me when they find a particular edition I am after.

So, is there snobbery in *Wisden* collecting? Indeed, is a collection only a true collection if it comprises completely original editions? In conversations with Bill Furmedge, he believes that there are probably no more than sixty or seventy completely original collections, comprising paperbacks to 1895 and hardbacks to present day, but there could be over 300 full collections comprising box sets, Billings, Willows, rebinds, paperbacks, linen cloth editions or hardbacks with or without dust jackets. In terms of the Almanack – the information, the articles, the descriptive narrative through three different centuries – is the owner of one of the 300 any less of a collector than the owner of one of the sixty or seventy?

With a limited supply of both the Wisden box set and the Billings editions, and with Willows also having a capped print run, this could mean that there might well be only around 2,000 1864s in any format in existence. Indeed, as Billings very rarely come up, a lot of those could well have been lost. The same could be said for the 1875.

I know that some people constantly upgrade, which is a policy that they follow, and for whatever reason it is their choice. Good luck to them. I presume this is done to enhance the value of a collection, but if that is the case I feel it is a false investment.

If I owned a full *Wisden* collection I am led to believe that on average whether selling via an auction or selling to a dealer, the amount I would receive would be between 40% and 50% of the sell-on price. Professional *Wisden* sellers are like any other business and I do not begrudge the industry a profit.

By upgrading my collection, am I not just upgrading to achieve a very small increment when I sell? Having a book in my collection bought for £100 and then upgrading to a better one at say £150 would actually mean that I would receive between £60 and £75, rather than £40 and £50: the extra investment does not justify the return. Simplistic, I know, and probably a little naive too, as I have taken no account of inflation, growth through scarcity etc. The *Wisden* dealer has access to the market and a database of potential customers, which a *Wisden* seller does not. Therefore unless you can find a *Wisden* dealer who will sell for as much as he can and take a small commission, the fact is that those who want to collect to invest are possibly misdirected.

Back to snobbery: the great thing about my collection is that I read them, I enjoy them, I refer to them, and the fact that many have pencil marks against players, little marks against scores, pages that are a little folded, spines that are flaky and jackets that are a little used, all this has no bearing on whether I can still lose myself for a couple of hours in the 1922 I bought in 2012 at auction. Is the batting of Hutton and Hammond or the bowling of Larwood, the wicket-keeping of Ames or the achievements of WG better recorded in an original hardback than in a rebind? Of course not!

There seems to be no snobbery in the auction room, but alas when paying I am often stuck behind someone who has bought half the lots, and when it is my turn to pay for my one item I am hastily dealt with so the chap who has bought a quarter of all the lots can be seen to next.

I am interested to learn if others feel there is snobbery in collecting. Maybe it is just me!

....

1928

I bought a 1928 hardback at a book fair in Reigate in 1996. I had collected sporadically, but finding the '28, in great condition, spurred me on. The price tag was £10, but I managed to barter that down to £7. I also picked up a 1970 and a 1971 from the same seller the following year, again making a nuisance of myself by offering £2 for both, original mint dust jackets *et al.* Sadly, the book fair never came back to Reigate, or if it did, they kept it quiet.

> Charles Kortright was frustrated
> He found 'The Doctor' quite demanding
> "Surely you're not leaving, Doctor?
> There is still one stump standing"!

....

1982

We were visiting my wife's parents for Christmas some time in the 1980s. When it came to present-opening time, I was presented with a package which contained a 1982 *Wisden*. As a collector I was pleased with my gift. A little while later my mother-in-law said "Look what I've just found" and presented me with another package which also contained a *Wisden*. This was followed a little later by another and another until, in total, I had received nine *Wisdens*. Five were from the 1950s, plus 1942, 1943, 1944 and 1945 (all linen cloth and all in very good condition).

My mother-in-law worked in a travel agents' next to a secondhand bookshop in Dartford town centre. She knew the owner and had an arrangement that she would have first pick of any *Wisdens* that came in. She acquired these for just £4 each. What a fantastic Christmas present, and made all the more memorable by the way that they just kept appearing during the day.

> Bridgetown 1981
> The crowd all hold their breath
> As Boycs departs after six great balls
> From Michael Holding, 'Whispering Death'

....

The best job in the world!
I bought my first *Wisden* at the age of 15, in 1990. I have every almanack since then, but only a handful before it, which is something I hope to rectify in the years ahead.

I have been fortunate to have acquired most of my *Wisdens* through my job, and have never made a concerted effort to backdate my collection. I do remember the thrill of buying my early almanacks from Blackwells on Broad Street in Oxford, where I grew up, and cycling the five minutes to the Parks to catch the start of the first-class season, usually in arctic conditions that made even turning the pages a hazardous business.

I would always head straight for the review of Northamptonshire's season, or the report of whichever Test match Allan Lamb had scored a hundred in. If England had played West Indies in the previous year, this usually meant I was spoiled for choice; if the opponents had been Pakistan, I barely bothered (Lamb averaged 12 against them).

The exception would be to read about Tests I had personally attended. I remember reliving through *Wisden's* pages the last day of the 1992 Lord's Test against Pakistan, who won after collapsing to 90-odd for 8 in pursuit of 140-ish. As it turned out, that happened to be Lamb's final Test.

(Lawrence Booth: the current Editor of *Wisden*)

> Wisden's like a world-class batsman
> A ton's a fine old score to pass
> But to kick on to 150
> Now that really shows your class!

....

1973
Whilst visiting north-west Sutherland in 2011, I purchased very cheaply (change from a tenner) a 1973 *Wisden* (without dust jacket but otherwise in good order) from the Loch Croispol Bookshop and Gallery near Durness.

This is the most north-westerly bookshop in mainland Britain (it's a six-hour drive north of Glasgow and only about ten miles from Cape Wrath) and about as far removed from cricket and mainstream British life as it is possible to find. I was neither seeking a *Wisden* at the time nor expecting to find one, but there, deep in Clan Mackay country, it was. I had a very modest run of *Wisden* at the time (1990s onwards) but my find was enough to encourage me to fill the gap back to 1973 and then to start travelling back in time.

....

1968

Every year for my birthday in May my parents bought me the new *Wisden*. Cricket was and is a passion in our family and my father had a full collection, which sadly he sold in 1984. I believe the first edition I received was 1968, a linen cloth that is in tatters now. After I married, the yearly almanack still came along, each and every May, until my father passed away in 2006; my mother had died in late 1999. The tradition of receiving each edition has now been continued by my wife.

....

1951

1951 was the first *Wisden* I bought, but it was purchased in error. In a tiny bookshop in Maidstone I had spotted a book in the sports section on motor racing. It was pretty tightly held on the shelf and to one side was the 1951 *Wisden*. My wife saw me with the *Wisden* and made a mental note that she would buy it as a surprise. I had little interest in cricket, and I had no idea what a *Wisden* was, but the other book was a great find. In the end I bought the motor racing book myself and my wife made an excuse that she had forgotten something and went back to get the 1951, thinking I wanted it.

I am glad she did. I spent more time poring over that than the other book, and as they say, thus it began.

....

1984

My anecdote relates to the first *Wisden* I acquired. It was the 1984 edition. This *Wisden* was available via my local library. As it was classified as a reference book, one could not borrow it but simply peruse in the library. As I flicked through the pages it captivated my attention; I had not seen a book of this type before.

At the time, Australia did not have a book of a similar type. I visited various bookshops but could not locate this edition or the current edition. Consequently, I decided to purchase the book from the library. Noting the Australian dollar price of the book, I placed the amount on the bookshelf where the 1984 *Wisden* was kept and took the book. I did feel a bit guilty but assuaged my conscience by the fact that I had left the cost of the book on the shelf.

This happened back in the late 1980s (1988 or 1989). Over the 20-plus years since, my collection has expanded to cover from 1938 to the current edition.

....

Not-so-easily distracted
My wife knows that if I pick up a *Wisden,* there is nothing to distract me from exploring its content, and she also knows that in early April there is nothing to stop me from eagerly opening the latest arrival.

"Go tell your dad the new Wisden has arrived"

Why we love Wisden

I am a cricketer: a cricketer in the heart, in the soul and in the spirit. The game of cricket still evokes passion in me, although my playing days are now sadly long over. One of cricket's outstanding siblings is *Wisden Cricketers' Almanack.*

With its uninterrupted issuance since it was first published in 1864, it has become the longest continuously printed sporting publication in history. Two bitter World Wars were unable to stop or contain it, although they did succeed in reducing its size throughout the years of their duration.

People say that cricket is dying; this theory has been mooted regularly from as far back as I can recall, and probably a lot further, but *Wisden* is certainly not dying. It grows in depth, and production runs have consistently increased.

Yes, cricket has changed and it continues to do so – this is how it maintains its good health. Its only tomb is the fabled Ashes, and what a splendid example of life that has proved to be. If *Wisden* were to shrink or fade, then concern should be shown that the great game is in decline.

Those of us who collect the cricketers' bible know it has been with us through thick and thin, or should I say thin to thick. It has had its crisis years when it was produced on sub-standard paper or was poorly bound; times when government restrictions curtailed print runs; arguments occurred over soft or hardbacks and changes in ownership and editorial.

In 1938 it was given a major shake-up; the soft linen cover was introduced and decorated with a timeless and elegant banner. This survived to become the face of *Wisden* for 65 years until 2003 when an unforeseen decision was taken to update, modernise but inadvertently downgrade its cover image. We are fortunate indeed that the publication itself is big and strong enough to withstand such undignified treatment.

There is a wonderful phrase in marketing which runs: "If it ain't broke, don't fix it." At the time *Wisden* was not broken and certainly didn't need fixing.

The *Wisden* brand carries with it considerable prestige, tradition, respect and responsibility. Its future editors should see themselves for what they are, the fortunate custodians of the great recorder, not it's driving force. Their prime tasks are to maintain its independence from cricket authorities and other predators, and to present the truth honestly, concisely and without favour, a difficult assignment which traditional *Wisden* editors never failed to understand.

Perhaps it is an increased element of journalism in its pages that has prompted some change. Editors should look to *Wisden's* history: it is not a jingoistic communicator of the game; it is a faithful document of fact and history; a complete record of the game's growth, activity and achievements; and by being thus it has earned its inherent strength and its appeal to all those people who love the game of cricket. It is indeed sport's most iconic publication.

> The sound of Test Match Special
> Makes the prefect summer day
> Think Arlott, Jonners, Blowers, Fred
> It's part of our DNA!

....

1898

My parents bought me a very good condition 1898 hardback (which I still have) for my twenty-first in 1977. I think it cost them around £70 then – not a bad investment! I first went to The Oval in July 1966 and my first *Wisden* was a 1967 covering that season. At the time I got the 1898 it was the earliest one I had by 68 years, but it certainly started the bug, and I now have a complete set, although a lot of them are Willows reprints.

....

Worth the wait

My first response when Monty Panesar and Matt Prior survived the last few overs against New Zealand in the Third Test of 2013 was elation. My second was: "What will *Wisden* make of it, I wonder?" And my third was: "Oh damn – I'll have to wait until spring 2014 to find out!" Against a 24-hour news barrage, *Wisden* offers a calm, considered perspective on exciting events and often febrile reactions to them. It is a wise custodian of so much of the game's heritage: personal and public, emotional and factual. It also means that summer is on the way!

> Down and out with a day to go
> The Kiwis had us on the floor
> But thanks to Matty P and Monty P
> We clung on for a draw !

....

I have to blame the 1967

My first *Wisden,* and thus the first 'brick' in my personal 'Yellow Brick Wall', was the 1967 edition. This was bought for me by my parents, at my instigation, as a present for my birthday that year. The general interest in cricket that had begun prior to my grammar school days was transforming into a fascination with, and collection of, cricket statistics that has been part of my life ever since.

I suspect that by then I had realised that I would never actually open the batting for Yorkshire and England, and should therefore channel my love of the great game into other cricket-related pursuits.

This particular *Wisden* will always be one of my sentimental favourites, as its battered and repaired covers testify. As I thumbed through it again prior to beginning these words, I realised that its subliminal impact on me is probably greater than I could ever have imagined.

I recently wrote an article for *The Wisdener* newsletter about the 1902 English season, nominating it as the season I would most have liked to have seen; one of the articles in the 1967 *Wisden* is 'My favourite summer' by that great Yorkshire cricket writer A. A. Thomson, and the summer in question? 1902, of course. I had completely forgotten about that article when I wrote that piece for *The Wisdener,* but somewhere in my subconscious mind the memory obviously lingered.

I did not start buying *Wisden* as it was published each year until the mid-1970s, which was a big mistake for reasons I will explain shortly, but soon after I began buying the Almanack each year the collecting instinct kicked in and I soon had the ambition of obtaining a complete run of *Wisdens* from the end of World War Two.

I remember purchasing a run of editions from the 1950s from J. W. McKenzie, but the great fun was hunting in secondhand bookshops for a *Wisden* that was not in my collection. These hunts were generally unsuccessful, which made the satisfaction even more enjoyable when another 'brick in the wall' was discovered and purchased.

One memorable find I owe largely to my wife, Ally. We lived in Headingley, and had walked down Kirkstall Lane to the junction with Kirkstall Road. Ally was browsing the window of an antiques/junk shop at the junction, looking for a bargain as always, and pointed out that there were a few of the familiar yellow-covered volumes in the shop window.

I had a look, expecting them to be fairly recent editions, but discovered three or four editions from the mid-1960s that were missing from my collection. Needless to say they were safely on our bookshelves that evening.

By the time Ally and I emigrated to Australia there was only one 'brick' remaining to complete my post-war run of *Wisdens.* The missing edition was 1971, which I now know can be particularly hard to find, apparently as fewer copies were printed than usual that year.

"You certainly know how to spoil a woman, darling"

I believe the explanation generally given as to why that happened is that there was no official Test series in 1970 due to the cancellation of the South African tour. I find that difficult to accept, as my strong recollection is that the 1970 Rest of the World versus England five-match series was marketed at the time as a fully-fledged Test series. Also, Alan Jones, the only new 'cap' to play for England in 1970, was thought to have achieved the status of being a Test player. Indeed, the list of England Test cricketers in each edition of *Wisden* from 1971 to 1979 lists Jones as having played one Test match, against the Rest of the World in 1970.

The hunt for the elusive 1971 *Wisden* continued through the secondhand bookshops of every Australian town and city visited, and my father also took it upon himself to look out for a copy back in England, using it as an excuse to visit towns far and wide from his home on the Yorkshire coast. By now I was, of course, kicking myself for not having started to buy *Wisden* each year from 1967 onwards.

The hunt finally ended on my first trip back to England, five years after emigrating. I had visited the Yorkshire CCC shop at Headingley and spotted a secondhand bookshop as I exited the ground via St Michael's Lane. I entered the shop for a browse, and could hardly believe my eyes as they were drawn to a yellow-covered volume of familiar dimensions. Could it possibly be? Yes, it could – a 1971 *Wisden* in perfect condition.

That particular bookshop is no longer to be found, and I am fairly sure that the location is now the home of the YCCC membership office, but whenever I visit Leeds I do tend to walk down St. Michael's Lane and say a silent thank you to whatever instinct or power guided me into that shop twenty years or so ago.

I continued collecting past editions of *Wisden* as and when they were spotted in various secondhand bookshops, and this activity picked up pace after Ally and I moved from our original Australian base in Canberra to Melbourne. The secondhand bookshops around Melbourne and Victoria's country towns are a delight and a treasure trove for any bibliophile, and it was something that we missed when we moved back to the Canberra region ten years later.

One find from our Melbourne days will always stand out from the pack. Once again, it must be admitted that my wonderful wife has to take the credit. Ally entered a shop on Swanston Street, in the heart of Melbourne, called 'Fabian's Fine Old Furniture'. It was difficult from the frontage to be quite sure what the shop was actually selling, but it turned out that the fine old furniture consisted of Fabian's desk, and the bookshelves containing an amazing collection of books for sale.

Fabian Hely himself was tall, slim and slightly eccentric, but a warm and gentle man who enjoyed talking about his books, and occasionally selling one. Ally spotted on the shelves a run of *Wisdens* from 1908 to 1916, all beautifully rebound. She negotiated an agreement that we would purchase one each month, and that Fabian would keep them for us in his store until we had bought the set. Over the months that we were buying the *Wisdens* from Fabian I also bought from him a number of Yorkshire CCC yearbooks from the 1950s, plus *Playfair* and *News Chronicle Cricket Annuals* from the 1950s and '60s.

The purchase from Fabian kicked off a new ambition to collect a complete set of *Wisdens* from the so-called 'Golden Age' of cricket from 1890 to 1914, an era in which I am particularly interested. *Wisdens* from this era are obviously hard to find via ad-hoc searches in secondhand bookshops in Australia, but after discovering the 'Wisdenworld' internet site in 2011 I have been able to take my run back to 1896, and also have the 1891 and 1892 editions, so hopefully will soon have the full 'Golden Age' set.

This will include a few Willows reprints, but personally I am more than happy to include these in my collection. I do not know if I will ever own a complete set of *Wisdens,* but it will not worry me unduly if I never achieve that particular milestone. I do know that I thoroughly enjoy the collection I already have and will continue to add to them. After the 1890 to 1914 run is complete I will add more volumes to those I already own from between the wars. For myself, the great joy of old *Wisdens* is to be able to read the contemporary reports and opinions about great cricketers and matches of bygone days and read the articles penned by the great cricket writers through the ages. They are definitely there to be read and referred to, not as an investment.

....

"Well done, my boy"

I inherited my grandfather's collection of *Wisdens*. He had them back to 1880. The nineteenth-century ones are mostly rebinds in various bindings, but the pick of the collection is an 1899 original hardback in quite good condition. But my personal favourite is a 1931 paperback, which was bought for him by his father, and inside there is a little note, which simply says: "Well done, my boy."

It may seem nothing special, nor was it cricket related, but my grandfather won the 100-yards dash on school sports day – no mean feat for an asthma sufferer – and his father had bought him the *Wisden* in celebration.

> The greatest ever cricket quote
> That an author could bestow?
> 'What do they know of cricket
> Who only cricket know'!

....

1982

My first *Wisden* was the 1982. I bought it to read about the Benson & Hedges Cup Final of 1981 that my dad had taken me to. We were supporting Surrey, but after seeing Garner and Richards dominate the game for Somerset I switched my allegiance – a difficult thing to do for a 13-year-old at a fervent cricket-playing school in Guildford.

> The best batsman that I ever saw?
> Viv Richards, 'Master Blaster'
> The only other who could get near?
> Tendulkar, 'Little Master'!

....

The ideal partner

When Andrew and I were dating, it became very apparent that one of his passions was cricket. Thankfully it's a subject I enjoy, especially having been involved as a social secretary and then secretary to a local cricket club in my twenties. I think he was a little stunned to know that I understood a lot of the game including field positioning, how Test matches work, even how to score a game using the traditional scoresheets.

When we moved in together in 2005, I inherited a lot of these little yellow books. He had been collecting *Wisden* since the mid-'70s, when he fell in love with the game, and I found a bookshelf that I could dedicate to them. I knew enough about *Wisden,* especially as my dad had collected some for a while, that it had been an almanack that started quite a number of years ago. So, I set about my research about how many were in existence and how to fill in some of the gaps in the collection.

He is also very interested in statistics generally and has developed his own spreadsheet using the *Wisdens* in his collection to do a new calculation on who could be defined as the top cricketers of all time.

Our first Christmas together was quite special. I had bought him three *Wisdens* from eBay, the first a very good condition 1970, which completed all the '70s series for him, a 1913 and a 1963. I remember him excitedly calling his dad on the day: "I've had my *Wisden* collection increased, the West Indies Tests of 1969 and the triangular tournament!"

He now has all the '60s, a lot of the '50s, a number of the '40s, '30s and a few of the '20s and war years, the set from 1864-1878 and some recent additions in the 1898 and 1900 Willows editions. It's always the first present on every Christmas, birthday or special occasion he makes a beeline for!

The blond-haired beach bum turns his arm
And it pitches way down leg
Fat Gatt is shocked as he looks behind
And sees it hit his off-stump peg!

"Oh Andrew, please let me keep score for the first eleven on Saturday"

....

A very easy present
I buy the *Wisdens* for my husband because he has been collecting them for
years, and I thought it would be a good source of presents to buy the earlier
ones for him. He gets a great deal of pleasure from dipping into them and the
one comment he made at Christmas was that he was getting even more pleasure
from the older ones because Yorkshire were doing so well!

....

An eventful hospital stay
I became interested in cricket when very young. At the age of five I was
hospitalised and sent to the Belgrave Hospital which was then opposite the Oval
Station. I'm told that I asked the doctor if I could be moved to a higher floor so
I could watch the cricket at The Oval.

In 1961, aged eight, I was taken to my first county game, and later that summer
I got taken to see England v Australia at The Oval. I never looked back:
summers were spent studying averages, reading newspaper reports and listening
to a transistor radio. In 1963 the West Indies were the tourists and someone my
father worked with said he could get him two tickets for Lord's. The problem
was it was Thursday, the first day. My father never condoned lying or deceit,
and told me he'd write to the headmaster of my school asking if it was
permissible for me to miss school to go to the Test match. Fortunately the head
wrote back saying that going to a Test match at Lord's should be a part of every
boy's education; I'm not sure that would happen today.

I had become a fervent Surrey supporter (I still am) and Mickey Stewart and
John Edrich were selected to open, while my boyhood hero Ken Barrington was
also in the team. However, the West Indies won the toss and batted. Little did I
know what a remarkable Test match it would be, primarily remembered for
Colin Cowdrey coming out to bat with a broken arm to prevent defeat.

By the next summer I had become a junior member at The Oval. There was a
bookstall by the side of the pavilion steps and I spent many an hour looking at
the books, photos and magazines. I was such a regular that on occasions the
owner asked me to mind the stall while he got food, drink etc.

To most eleven-year-olds, *Wisden* would not seem instantly appealing, but one
day at the stall I opened a copy and discovered it was full of statistics, averages
and details: I was transfixed.

I saved up and bought the 1964 edition because it had the details of my first
visit to Lord's, and the rest of a season that I had studied in such depth. I still
have that hardback edition, although sadly the dust jacket disintegrated over the
years. Looking at it now it shows the impact of that West Indian tour: the Five

Cricketers of the Year are Hunte, Kanhai, Griffiths, Sobers and the defiant Brian Close.

I didn't realise at the time, but it had within it a wonderful obituary and statistical record of England's finest batsman, Sir Jack Hobbs, written by Neville Cardus. *Wisden* 1964 sowed the seed, and now its appearance in April lets me know that summer and cricket will soon be here.

A quiet day in Swansea
Until Sir Garry got his fix
By hitting poor old Malcolm Nash
For a six-ball thirty-six!

....

Dipping into Wisden

For me the joy of *Wisden* lies in its broad timespan rather than the contents of each individual almanack. I was fortunate to build up a healthy collection during the late 1970s while copies were still available from secondhand bookshops and local auction houses at reasonable prices.

As the collection grew, I gained considerable pleasure tracing the careers of postwar cricketers from first reference in *Wisden* to later famous deeds. Colin Cowdrey's remarkable first performance at Lord's as a 13-year-old for Tonbridge in 1946 with both bat and ball was promise indeed, and in the twilight years 151 not out for Kent to defeat the Australian tourists, including Chappell, Lillee, Walters *et al* in 1975. And so many achievements for England in between times.

Research into earlier periods revealed longer careers. Archie MacLaren announced himself at the top of the Harrow batting averages in the 1888 *Wisden* (1887 season at the age of 16) and then kept appearing with frequency and style: 424 for Lancashire against Somerset at Taunton in 1895, leading an England XI to victory over Warwick Armstrong's 1921 Australians at Eastbourne, and signing off with 200 not out for MCC against New Zealand at Wellington in 1922/23. This was the first of three encounters that winter between MCC and New Zealand, described by *Wisden* as "dignified with the name of Test Matches".

As a keen follower of sport, but cricket and football in particular, I used to listen avidly to the radio sports quiz, 'Brain of Sport', on a Saturday evening, hosted by sports clubs from around the country. The late Peter Jones was the question-master and contestants selected a sport about which they would be asked five questions. They were usually challenging and good fun to attempt at home. In one programme, cricket was chosen and one of the questions was: "Who was the only person to play first-class cricket in England before the outbreak of the

First World War and after the end of the Second World War?" Neither the recipient of the question nor I could provide the answer, which was W. H. (Bill) Ashdown of Kent.

This, I thought, was worthy of research among my recently acquired run of *Wisdens*. References to Births and Deaths revealed that Ashdown was born on December 27, 1898. This meant that he was only 15 during the 1914 season and 47 in the summer of 1946. My first inclination was to ring the BBC and tell them that they had the question wrong!

As with every dip into *Wisden*, the eye readily wanders and the mind drifts into other trains of thought. I mused on the influence that Asif Iqbal had on the maturing of Pakistan as a Test-playing country, the emergence of one-day cricket and the role of the overseas player in county cricket.

Was Ewart Astill really born in 1888 and still playing cricket for Leicestershire in his 52nd year? That brought me back to the matter in hand and the possibility that the question was correct.

Delving into various volumes of *Wisden* and other books provided some facts about Ashdown. He was a prolific opening bat in the 1920s and 1930s with 1,000 runs a season 11 times, two 300s and a county career that spanned 1920 to 1937. All the facts pointed to an honest inter-war county career for a reliable professional batsman. Consulting the 1915 *Wisden*, I was determined to find this 15-year-old debutant, but where to start?

There was no hint of any connection with Kent at this stage. It had to be an MCC game or some 'other match' with first-class status at the end of the Golden Age.

This avenue of exploration was fruitless, but following a similar line of thought I glanced through the university matches to find Oxford's final home fixture against G. J. V. Weigall's side. Batting at number six was W. Ashdown, one of two professionals in the team. He scored 27 in the second innings, prompting *Wisden* to comment: "On Wednesday, Ashdown, a lad of 15, showed considerable promise." He also bowled 16 overs for 54 runs and no wickets in what turned out to be Oxford University's only innings.

Applying the same principle to the post-Second World War season of 1946 should easily have revealed Ashdown's involvement in first-class cricket for that year. Alas, no joy whatsoever! But 1947 provided the answer. Ashdown opened the batting for Maurice Leyland's XI against The Rest during the end-of-season Harrogate Festival. He scored 42 and 40 and took five wickets for 73 runs – and all this after ten years away from first-class cricket.

It took many hours of totally pleasurable, often distracted, research to find the correct answer to this obscure question. Ironically, Bill Ashdown died in September 1979 and the 1980 *Wisden* with its impeccable attention to detail told the story from the odd beginning to the end of his first-class career in his obituary.

The delight of *Wisden* is to rummage in one volume, then another and another.

(The above article is reproduced with the kind permission of David Jennings of Willows Publishing. It first appeared in *The Journal of The Cricket Society,* Volume 18, Number 4, Spring 1998.)

....

1988

My first *Wisden* was the 1988 edition, and picking it off the shelf now, it is quite a curious read.

The Notes by the Editor probably reflect the state that the game was in. Graeme Wright was the editor and he covers 21 topics in his notes, including substitutions, umpiring controversy and player dissent. In many ways, not a lot has changed in the game, but his notes seem to be surrounded by doom, gloom and despondency.

Even the weather was awful in 1987 and all the county teams were involved in a large number of draws. England were involved in a dull five-match series against Pakistan that featured four draws and a defeat.

During the ODI element of that tour I also had the misfortune to be at the third game at Edgbaston where a fantastic game won by England by one wicket was marred by crowd trouble.

So why should I have started my collection in 1988 when apparently there weren't many positives to draw upon? The secret lies between pages 906 and 929 where England's tour to Australia is covered. England retained the Ashes and also won one-day tournaments, and don't forget the largely forgotten win in Sharjah as well.

Perhaps *Wisden* covering the entire Ashes tour in 23 pages illustrates how the game has changed in terms of media coverage. By comparison, the 2011 Almanack reported the latest tour in 39 pages.

I would never pick *Wisden* 1988 as one of my favourites, but it was my opener and therefore has a special place in my collection. Since 1988 my interest in the Almanack has flourished and my collection now covers from 1971 to date.

It may be a drop in the ocean to a lot of collectors, but I am thrilled with what I have achieved to date. The big question now, I suppose, is do I go back to the '60s and beyond – and the answer to that has got to be yes. There is so much magic to uncover!

Stanford flirted with the ECB
They simply blushed and said, 'That's nice!'
Just proves that everyone's a courtesan
It's just a question of the price!

....

My Wisdens

The natural and predictable question whenever I show anyone around my library is: "Do you have a full set of *Wisden?*" And the answer has to be slightly equivocal. Yes, I do have a complete run – although many are facsimiles.

There are two reasons for this. First, it would have cost far more than I was ever prepared to pay to acquire a full set of originals, even allowing that when I started, around sixty years ago, many of the earlier editions were still available fairly cheaply. I think Auntie Edie, back in the 1950s, paid around £2 for a 1927 when I fancied the one covering England's historic 1926 Ashes victory.

The fact is, at one point I had almost a full run, including the first boxed facsimile set of the first fifteen (1864-1878). Then as Willows facsimiles appeared, they filled the gaps and also took the place of originals.

Unlike many a *Wisden* collector, I actually work regularly with my set, researching for books and features, or simply enjoying the read. (The *Wisdens* of some years ago were nowhere near as accurate as today's compilations, nor as enjoyable a read. Tucked into my 1905 volume is a cutting of Sir Home Gordon's letter to *The Sportsman* listing errors and omissions for that particular edition: I've continued to apply corrections wherever possible.)

There are certain originals I would never want to part with in favour of a facsimile, and you'll probably see why when I explain. Firstly, there's the 1951 *Wisden,* which was my own first copy. Among my tonnage of books today, this is probably the most sentimentally prized volume of them all, inscribed as it is in my boyish hand. But over the years I've been fortunate enough to acquire some very special *Wisdens.*

In the late 1960s, when researching the life of A. E. Stoddart, England's much-loved and glamorous captain in the first great Test series (1894/95), my researches led me to a man who had acquired some of 'Stoddy's' possessions many years earlier. I was speechless with joy when he let me have the great man's signed 1892 *Wisden.* Many years later, for a steep price at auction, I added Stoddart's 1896 *Wisden,* this one featuring his pencilled notes comparing the figures of his bowlers on his 1894/95 and 1897/98 tours of Australia. What sublime joy it is for a biographer to handle such gems as these.

In between the two Stoddart *Wisdens* I acquired three delicate, slim *Wisdens* which had once been owned by the champion hitter G. L. Jessop (how 'The Croucher' would have enjoyed Twenty/20 cricket). They are limp-covered editions for 1879, 1880 and 1881, and yet again the fingers tend to tremble just handling them. They aren't signed by Jessop, but the provenance is impeccable: a letter from the man from whom I bought them, Jessop's son.

Equally special are two *Wisdens* (1914 and 1915) once owned and handled by Percy Jeeves, one of the most renowned casualties of the First World War, a Warwickshire player who had seemed certain to become a Test cricketer. Percy was proud of his bowling achievements. The best of them he has underlined. I'm reminded of an observation made recently by a friend: "These books have his DNA all over them!" This rare pair of *Wisdens* came via his generous brother Harold.

Another of my *Wisdens* which has a famous association is the 1938, bought from Syd Smith junior, long-time NSW and Australian Board secretary and manager of the 1921 and 1926 tours of England. In the garage I also have his enormous cabin trunk, with its yellowing 'Ashes' label still stuck on. But that's another story.

Tucked into the books themselves are contemporary reviews and published comment, embracing among other things the tragi-comic Iranian Embassy siege in 1984, when dinner-jacketed diners insisted on pushing past the police cordon. Nothing interferes with the *Wisden* dinner, the constables and snipers were told.

Next to the shelves loaded with *Wisdens* is a bundle of other material relating to the Almanack and its long-ago founder: two published indexes, cuttings, letters, leaflets, a picture I took of the ceramic Wisden shop plaque in Cranbourn Street in London, and associated coverage of events such as the 1984 unveiling of John Wisden's brand new memorial on his grave in Brompton Cemetery on the centenary of his death.

The shelves full of *Wisdens* are but one frontage in an extensive library, but they remain a focal point. Many a visitor has seemed to be transfixed by the rows of yellow and brown gold-blocked spines. And many have not been able to resist embarking on a little bit of research themselves, seeking the editions in which their names are to be found.

Sometimes it is for an isolated county match but more often it is to find the name in the Schools Cricket section. Forget your Stoddarts, Jessops and

Jeeveses: it seems that this fleeting piece of print somehow convinces a man that his life has been worthwhile.

David Frith (Mr Frith founded *Wisden Cricket Monthly* magazine in 1979 and edited it until 1996 and has written many books on Cricket)

....

1916

I go through phases over which *Wisden* is my favourite. If I had to choose one, and being honest, it would be chosen for mainly non-cricketing reasons, it would be the 1916. It does contain the obituary and career records of WG and the obituaries of Trumper and Stoddart, but for me it is the contrast between the wonderful, amazing, sensational, detailed life of the man who did more for the game than any other, and the page after page of those who had fallen in World War One – those who did not get the opportunity to make their mark. Sitting with a tot of my favourite single malt and thumbing through the pages of my 1916 is very humbling.

....

My Other Woman

My wife tells friends that I have been having an affair for years with a woman called *Wisden*. She says that there is nothing she can do to drag me away from this harlot!

"What has Northamptonshire v Derbyshire got that I haven't?"

My wife's a book collector
She's got those 'Fifty Shades of Grey'
You can forget your whips and 'house of pain'
I'll stick with Wisdens any day!

....

Cricket and Wisden in the Colonies: A young lad's memories
The cricket interest is from my father's side of the family. His first years were
spent in Lima, Peru. This was the same time when a young lad called Freddie
Brown was also living in Lima, Brown being born in 1910 and my father in
1912. My grandmother says she gave Freddie Brown his first cricket bat. Truth
or fiction, it was a possibility. Suffice to say that neither my father nor young
Freddie would have had too much difficulty with the local new-ball attack – at
least until the ball hit the surface.

The family repatriated to England and then migrated to New Zealand after
World War Two. Cricket was always on the agenda. In New Zealand in the
1950s (and still today) there was no shortage of land. The front lawn of a
normal suburban home could provide a 22-yard strip, a bowler's run-up of ten
yards at one end, and a fence at the other that 'kept wicket'. Gender played a
part – boys could bat and bowl, girls could field. Rules, particularly for
dismissals, were influenced by seniority.

The first footage of a cricket match on television was in the mid 1960s.
Occasionally, at the cinema, a world news coverage might feature up to a
minute of highlights from a game played in England. Media exposure was
newspapers and radio. Newspapers reported at length, in detail, and if it was in
the paper, it was the truth. Radio tried to entertain with sensation and drama –
but this was 'ordinary', first-class, New Zealand domestic fare – of which, in
the late 1950s, there were 15 games in the whole season. If an overseas team
was touring, there would naturally be more games. But, due to the standard of
cricket, and the standard of wickets, overseas teams were infrequent visitors.

The highlight of cricket via the media was whenever an overseas team toured
Australia. With a time difference of two hours, stumps would be drawn at 8.00
pm New Zealand Time. If we attached a wire to the back of the radio and
hooked it around metal items in proximity, and switched the band to short-
wave, we could pick up intermittent commentary, generally of the post-tea
session.

The series I remember the most – actually there were two of them – was the
West Indies in 1960/61, and England in 1962/63. The 'Tied Test' was as much
remembered for losing the broadcast signal in what was the last over, as it was
for the result itself. Editing deadlines had passed, so we had to wait until the
evening paper 24 hours later to know what the result was. The other was one of
the Tests when England was in Australia in 1963. My father had his views on
the selection process for some of the English players – and, as children of the
1950s and 1960s, father's views were (sensibly) our views as well. There was
an English player whom father felt should not have been in the team, not in any
team – but should have been attending to his profession, i.e. tending his flock
(and not as a farmer). My recollection is that in the space of a few overs, the

player in question dropped two catches. Without the benefit of television and egged on by the cawing of the Australian commentators, the catches were 'dollies' and should have been taken. The offender had confirmed, once and for all, that he did not belong in the team. And we believed it to be the case as well. Mother, who was born near Reigate, was less sure – a significance I learned only later in life.

In the few years prior to the West Indies' tour of Australia, my father noticed that I was easily entertained by reading the scoreboards of any games reported in the newspapers. I had a penchant for arithmetic. Once I understood the meaning of OMRW, that 'Not Out' did not increase the divisor for a batsman's average, that records existed for all sorts of achievements, I would pore over clippings and extracts for hours, trying to see who was improving an average, who bowled the most maiden overs etc.

It was then that father introduced me to *Wisden*. He told me about this book where all the records were kept, all the scores of first-class matches – everything one might want to know. I biked the five miles to the main library in Christchurch to see if they had a copy. Eventually, such a publication was located in the records. But there was a problem. It was classified as 'Reference' and therefore was in the 'Reference Section'. A lad of nine was too young to be in the 'Reference Section'. A lad of nine could not reach the shelf in question. A lad of nine would not be allowed to use the 'Librarian's Ladder'. A lad of nine, a sad lad, biked five miles home, not even having seen what this book looked like, not even being allowed in the room where it was kept.

But fathers can do anything. Dad worked with a man called 'Curly' Page (M. L. Page). Mr Page was a deity in New Zealand. Mr Page had played cricket for New Zealand (once scoring a century at Lord's v England); more importantly, Mr Page had played rugby for New Zealand – an All Black. And, yes, Mr Page was happy to help a young lad of nine get access to the Reference Section at the Christchurch Public Library.

And, so about a week later, we received a letter from the library saying that I should present myself with a parent and the library's letter to discuss books of interest in the Reference Section. Mother thought the occasion demanded full school uniform, tie and cap.

Father and son duly arrived. We presented ourselves and the library letter and were introduced to two very serious ladies who were interested more in why a lad of nine would want to read *Wisdens*.

On reflection, and subsequently learning that the copies in the library had not moved from their shelf for as long as either of the two very serious ladies could remember, this peculiar situation of a lad of nine and some hitherto unread books (whose lack of patronage had seen them go up to the highest shelf possible) was of great interest.

Perhaps it was bemusement, the possible unveiling of some strange interest, or just a fascination with the bizarre request, but the two very serious ladies seemed satisfied that I was of sufficient character and manner to be given access to the Reference Section. However, I was to sit at the reading-desk directly in line of sight of the Supervisor, I was not to take any books from shelves, I was confined to *Wisdens,* I was not to mark the books in any way – but I could copy material if I wanted to, a concession, I am sure, that was granted without any expectation that such copying by hand would eventuate.

Father and I were installed in the Reference Section that day – just as well, because I was asked which one did I want to read. Father said: "Let's get the lad the one where Mr Laker took the 19 wickets." Asserting ever so slightly, given our seemingly probationary status, father went on to say that the game in question was in 1956 so that would be the *Wisden* of 1957. That was never going to be enough information for the very serious lady. "On the top shelf up there, small, thick, yellow book, look for the numbers 1957 or 95," suggested father.

The book was found; it was brought down to us, and a reminder about care and privilege was delivered. "And that, my son, is a *Wisden* – the cricketer's Bible." Father showed me how to read the book – in simple terms, that is – looking more for points of interest as much as anything else.

Then, as we made our way to the Fourth Test with Laker's 19-wicket haul, my father took an interest in some statistics – one of those moments when a parent might be reading to a child and the voice trails off as the parent reads only for him/herself.

He was at that part of the book where it showed scorers of over 1,500 runs in Test matches, or bowlers with more than 75 wickets (in preparing this essay I note these as pages 180 and 181). And here the reality and context of New Zealand in the cricketing world sat starkly in front of me. One New Zealander only – only one New Zealander – Bert Sutcliffe for batting.

I leant forward on my elbows toward the book (and the very serious lady seemed to stop what she was doing, surprised perhaps that there was some real interest emerging) and asked my father why there was only one New Zealander, when there were so many players from other countries with more than 1,500 runs, and more than 75 wickets. I recall the answer being "many reasons" but then father started to talk about the players who were in the lists – the records they had set along the way, the highest scores etc. Father said that in years to come there would be more New Zealanders in the lists and it could be interesting to keep track of them.

Interesting it was. As, too, was the way in which my father propagated my education in the contents of *Wisdens*. As a treat – and it was a treat – he would set me questions. "What is the highest score in any form of the game by a batsman?" "What was significant about J. W. Burke in that Test at Old Trafford?" "Who bowled the most deliveries in a Test match?" And on they'd go – each time a trip to the library where, by now, I was quite welcome (a year had passed since holding my first *Wisden*), and one of the staff in the Reference Section had a passing interest in cricket and was fascinated at the information one could glean.

I would copy down various records for my own home-made *Wisdens:* we were not particularly well-off financially as a family, so the thought of actually owning my own copy never entered my head. But that all changed on my eleventh birthday.

....

1934
My favourite *Wisden* is my 1934, a hardback purchased from a dealer around 1998. I was always aware it was the 'bodyline' edition and so I knew it would be expensive, but that wasn't the primary reason for buying it. It contained the first cricket match my dad ever saw, England v the West Indies at Old Trafford and he always waxed lyrical over Headley's 169 in the first innings for the tourists. It is a very small link to my dad, but reading about the match in *Wisden* and knowing he had been in the crowd means so much.

....

Memory Man
My father always remembered birthdays and anniversaries by connecting them to some world event. Well, so he said, but a few years after he died my mother came to stay for Christmas and she had us in hysterics telling us how he actually remembered important family dates.

My wife asked, what link did he put on our wedding day, July 2, and quick as a flash my mother said: "His best mate got his first hundred for the club." She then went through the entire family, my three brothers, their children, their wedding days, my sisters, the same for them, and even, much to our surprise, distant relatives we hardly ever saw.

"Of course I remember our wedding day, Edna. Big Jim got a five-four at Sawtry"

Buying Wisdens the traditional way

My Wisdening stories may not be too romantic or dramatic to others, but I've enjoyed the 'journey' so far in garnering my collection of 71 editions. I've managed to avoid the instant and somewhat unsatisfactory clinical purchasing by eBay and indeed have not bought online at all. I've found, as with many things in life, that the instant and 'must have now' world is not necessarily an ideal one, since I grew up without it and in a world wherein you bought what you needed and not a lot more! I do keep a record, though, of my source of purchase, price paid, condition and an arbitrary grading system out of ten for the book overall, even though it is handwritten on a fairly tatty piece of paper.

My first purchase was a 1977 at the age of 14, which I finally bought after walking into Newark Bookshop (long since disappeared and now a bed centre) every Saturday for weeks and studying it lovingly before telling my parents I wanted to buy it: £3.50 I think it was. I bought odd copies as the years went by, filling the gaps when I moved into my own home and therefore feeling less of a geek, or rather only a geek to myself! A lot of my 1950s, 1960s and early 1970s were bought from Peter Wynne-Thomas's shop 'Sport in Print' situated opposite Trent Bridge, until it closed a few years ago. I think I had a whole plastic bag full after one visit – there must have been at least 15, that I think were part of a house clearance.

I, like many others, regarded it as the best shop in England, a veritable Aladdin's cave of new and used books, magazines, programmes and ephemera that could keep anyone of a mind occupied for hours on end. Many a time have

I missed most of the afternoon session of a Notts match looking at the over-stocked shelves. A truly sad day when it closed – I felt a part of my life had gone. PWT used to run his Association of Cricket Statisticians and Historians affairs from the back room. He is still great friends with my brother (who conveniently works at Trent Bridge) and we swap questions and trivia by text now, with my brother being the 'middle man'. PWT is a wonderful, knowledgeable man, affectionately known as 'The Professor' or just 'Prof'.

My 1938 (very smart with bat bookmark intact) and 1949 hardback were bought from Border Bookshop in Todmorden, a shop I always visited whenever I was close by on business. This is another marvellous shop. A more organised version of PWT's shop but great for secondhand *Wisdens* and cricket books (and other sports and comics). Prices are strong, but I don't mind paying them in the right circumstances. Shops like this have to make a living or they disappear – and many have in recent years as we give in to eBay and online purchases. The beauty of collection is in the chase and covet and then decision to buy, surely? A press of the 'send' button when ordering online just doesn't compare.

The 1940, 1941 and 1942 I have are Willows reprints: the 1940 I got from William Roberts along with a 1947 from Christopher Saunders at York Racecourse Bookfair a few years ago, although I paid more than I would have wished. I love the 1946 softback I have from Sport in Print – in good nick, and like the others from that period (I've a 1948 rebind also), a real microcosm of postwar life and austerity, the 1948 a fascination with its browned pages from around halfway through.

The 1948 bebind was another I coveted (sounds rather biblical or libidinous?) in Geoff Blore's Bookshop in Nottingham a few years ago, seeing it one Friday afternoon without any cash on me and driving back there the next morning to get it with a rather spurious excuse to my wife for the journey's purpose.

Another *Wisden* that had to spend a few days in my car boot before being smuggled on to the shelves! This is another bookshop I visit when I can (along with Jermy & Westerman a little further down Mansfield Road) because of its great selection of cricket books – your typical old-style bookshop with electric bar heater, worn-out carpets and literally (pardon the pun) thousands of books to look over.

I'm always slightly disappointed with the 1950s, not just *Wisden*-wise (a new word perhaps?) but generally. This was the decade that brought us rock 'n' roll and pastel shades, but everything appears so austere and colourless looking back. Maybe it was just the back end of rationing and the postwar rebuilding of society that taints our viewpoint, but in cricketing terms it was the pre-limited overs / one-day period and a decade of turgid, risk-free cricket that couldn't move with the moving times that seals it for me.

My 1950-59 *Wisdens* even appear like that on the shelves – a boring decade if ever there was one! Thankfully they give way to the bulging, over-paged 1963 with its bowed spine (I've not seen many that are unbowed – I've read they used the wrong glue to bind them?) and the coloured date-printing of the 1960s and early '70s.

I'm conscious I may be waffling now, and appreciate your time if you've got this far! I hope to augment my collection in due course; however, finances may conspire against me.

I would love to complete the 1919-1939 and WW2 years, as I think they're part of a fascinating period, and my real regret now is not commencing with the Willows reprints more earnestly when I could have done: £60 or £70 every few months wouldn't have been a hardship, although the justification to my wife would have been. Maybe I could have used the "it's my little avenue of pleasure" tagline, but it only works for so long.

....

1911

Asking me what *Wisden* means to me is simple. The first one I bought was a 1911 paperback, purchased in February1981 from a bookshop on Tottenham Court Road in London. It wasn't at all bad for its age: the covers were a little grubby but I was pleased with my £22 outlay.

I actually have no idea why I bought it. The 1910 season or the 1911 year held no significance to me – I just saw an old cricket book and I decided to buy it.

Thinking back, it sat on a bookshelf for ages at home, unread and unloved. It wasn't until I heard a radio report during the summer on a Worcestershire batsman, Turner, hitting 300 in a day and the announcer saying that "no doubt that will be in *Wisden*" that I remembered the 1911. I picked it up and the rest, as they say, is history. My collection was completed in early 2013 with the acquisition of a rather lovely 1869.

....

How I built my Wisden collection
I was fielding in the slips for Crowborough on a Wednesday afternoon friendly
match in the summer of 1981. At second slip, a friend said: "Derek, do you
collect Wisden?" "Why do you ask?" I replied. "Oh, because I bought a few
advertised in the Friday Ad (our local free paper) last week," he said.

These comments set me thinking, and on returning home that evening I lined up
my *Wisdens* on the kitchen table. I had a run from 1965 (the first year I bought a
Wisden) to 1981. This was not a large run but it did cover Kent's glory years
from the late 1960s to the late 1970s. Then I thought about trying to trace the
career of my boyhood hero Colin Cowdrey through the pages of *Wisden* and
realised that I would need a run commencing with 1946. Only then would I be
able to trace that illustrious career from Tonbridge to Test match.

Obtaining the copies from 1946 to 1964 was not difficult as I was able to
purchase these from general book dealers at modest prices, and within a couple
of months I had a complete run from the end of the Second World War to 1981.
Whenever I travelled to another town on school or family business, I always
made a point of visiting the secondhand bookshops, and in late 1982 I made
contact with Christine and Robert Swift who ran a secondhand bookshop in
Maidstone. I asked them to ring me whenever they had any *Wisdens* prior to
1946 in the shop.

Yes, you have guessed it: within a few days Robert rang to say that they had a
run of softbacks from 1920 to 1939. The asking price was £200 (today it would
be £2,000) and Robert would be quite willing to accept my collection of
Gillingham Football Club programmes in part exchange. Parting with the
Gillingham programmes was a wrench but cricket had become my number one
sport: I had to acquire these *Wisdens* as I would now possess all the cricket
between the two wars with the exception of 1939. (By the way, I have been a
Gills supporter for 60 years and saw my first game in 1953. Some of us have
our burdens to carry in life.)

A couple of weeks later Robert acquired 1940 to 1945 in linen covers. Actually,
I believe he always had them but just kept them back so that I could have my
appetite whetted again. Yes, another run appeared later in the year (1899 to
1914) and with the agreement of my wife Sheila and the bank manager I paid
for them with a £250 loan. So by late 1982 I had a run from 1899 to 1982 with
the exception of the war years 1915 to 1919 inclusive.

At about this time a friend suggested that a new *Index to Wisden* was needed
and I approached Macdonald and Jane's (owned by Robert Maxwell) to see if
they were interested in my idea. They were, so I needed access to all the other
Wisdens.

Martin Wood from Sevenoaks very kindly supplied 1916 and spread payment over three months, and the other war years were bought via the specialist dealers like John Mackenzie and John Eastwood. Facsimiles of the 1864 to 1878 issues were obtained from John Eastwood (these had belonged to comedian Tony Hancock's brother Roger) and reading copies of 1879 to 1898 from other collectors like Carl Openshaw who had spares. I did not mind the condition of the books – they just had to be readable. Over the years I have gradually replaced the softbacks with original hardbacks but this has now become a very expensive business. Recently an original hardback sold for £20,000 at auction.

Collectors of *Wisden* were dealt an excellent hand when the Willows Publishing Company decided to do reprints from 1879. These volumes are gradually increasing in value as all of them have been produced in a limited print run of usually 500 copies.

So today I possess a complete run thanks to the forbearance of my wife and the bank manager who was always willing to help. Friends have helped me by directing me to shops and sometimes even putting a deposit on a book until I could go and inspect it. No, I have not read every *Wisden* from cover to cover – I do intend to do so in the near future – but I think I know as much as anyone about the "Cricketer's Bible".

And the bargain buy? An 1874 original which I bought in a bookshop in Rye in 1984 for £4 and the lady apologised about the price!

Derek Barnard

....

1964: Such modest beginnings
Whenever we see a politician being interviewed in front of bookshelves groaning under the weight of bound copies of parliamentary proceedings, I always ask my wife, "Are they *Wisdens*?", such is the place the Cricketers' Almanack holds in our household.

My love affair with these books extends back much further than that with my wife, almost 50 years now, and produces a new offspring every year to go along with older generations acquired to complete the full set.

I was in my last year of primary school when the incessant pestering of my parents had the required effect of a much-sought-after Christmas present, the 101st edition. I had seen the book in a Launceston (Tasmania) bookshop earlier in the year, and was fascinated with its content. I had also been given a copy of E. W. Swanton's *The Ashes in Suspense* (covering the MCC's tour of Australia in 1962/63) in which Bernard Hollowood's introduction contained the tongue-in-cheek confession that he memorised whole tracts of *Wisden* while he was waiting for radio reports of the Test matches on that tour. Such was my innocence that I believed this and sought to emulate him. It was my constant companion in those summer holidays, and accompanied me to Hobart when I was packed off to boarding school in the New Year.

My parents were unwilling to outlay further funds to buy for me what they considered to be exactly the same book when the next editions were published, and it required me to save up to buy my next copy, the 1967 edition. Since then, it has been an automatic purchase for me. Much more fun has been the quest to go back in time and acquire older editions.

Entering the workforce as a teacher gave me the relative wealth to successfully attain my first goal, to get them all back to World War Two, mainly thanks to the doyen of Australian booksellers, Roger Page.

Not satisfied with this, the next task was to get the interwar editions, and for this I had to write to England, where E. K. Brown proved an amenable seller. I also bought the facsimile production of the first fifteen editions, which made obtaining the rest of the set a natural progression.

John McKenzie at Ewell was very helpful in getting me originals back to 1890. Anything before that seemed prohibitively expensive, and I was quite satisfied to buy the cheaper facsimiles for the 1880s to complete my collection nearly 20 years ago.

Given its many different sources, it would be considered something of a hotchpotch – a mixture of yellow and brown soft-covers interspersed with an array of different-coloured hard-cover rebindings. It would not be considered an elegant collection by dedicated bibliophiles, but it is a much-loved working collection that is frequently consulted, and it is obviously the centrepiece of my cricket book library.

Apart from that first 1964 copy, two editions are special to me: the 1883 edition, offered to me by Roy Darling, a neighbour, and son of Joe; and the rare 1916 volume, previously belonging to the New Zealand writer Arthur Carman.

A decade ago, we bought a beach house on the Tasmanian East Coast. Fearing withdrawal symptoms if I was to spend extended time away from my *Wisdens* at home, I kept a number of duplicate copies there, and these were reinforced in time by the purchase of a large number of post-WW2 duplicates from a local library.

At the same, I became aware of the good work done by David Jenkins in producing the Willows facsimiles, truly beautiful books that are much more robust than my originals. So it was that I kept pace with David's production schedule, and just last year secured my 149th volume for the holiday venue.

I have always been fascinated by the English county game, an interest that was initially stimulated by that first *Wisden* in 1964. I do feel that in its desire to cover the rapidly-burgeoning international game, *Wisden* has moved away from its original charter of covering the domestic game as comprehensively as it should.

In my retirement, I have provided the data for a computer database that a colleague and I distribute to a growing number of commercial and hobbyist clients, and we have been sure to provide in it the scorecards of those English limited-overs matches that *Wisden* no longer publishes.

I have been blessed recently by the birth of my first grandchild, a boy who will carry my surname into another generation. No one in my family was surprised when I announced that my first present to him would be … a copy of the 2013 *Wisden*. I couldn't imagine a better gift to carry him through his childhood.

....

Preaching to the converted
Whenever I pick up a copy of *Wisden,* no matter what year it relates to, it never ceases to amaze me that I can always find something of interest to read.

My first 'scan' takes me to the notes concerning the previous season's county details. This I do as it gives me a feel for "who done what (and sometimes, who didn't)", reading through each in turn from Derbyshire to Yorkshire. I find that exercise in itself stimulates my mind – with the result that I find myself muttering under my breath "Ooh, I remember that well" or "I don't remember that" or sometimes "How on earth could I forget that?"

Every now and again my eyes light up when I stumble upon a gem, such as a few years back when I was reading one of the obituaries in the 1994 edition which concerned Herbert Montandon Garland-Wells (1907-1993). I have no need to go into details, as it would be a case of 'preaching to the converted'.

My reason for being 'all of a flutter' is that I had been engaged at that phase in my life in researching my family history. For some time whilst working on that project, I had often wondered about the truth of some of our many family legends.

One of these was the subject of intense curiosity on my part. It had nothing whatsoever to do with a blood relative, but concerned the statement made on several occasions by my father (who hid his interest in my own humble cricketing exploits), that "Uncle Tod has a nephew who played cricket for

Oxford University". And that is as much as I knew up to the very day that I first skimmed through the 1994.

....

1949

My grandfather took me to Southend to watch the Australian touring team take on Essex on Saturday, May 15, 1948. It was the first day of the match. Sixty-five years later I must tell you about my residing memory of that day. It isn't of Bradman, Saggers, Brown or Loxton all scoring centuries in a day, nor is it the Aussie score of 721, again in a day. It isn't the applause that greeted both Bradman and Miller as they walked on to the field and the standing ovation that all the players received as they left the field. Not any of that, which I have subsequently read about in books, including *Wisden*. No, it is the fact that because I did not take my hat and coat, as my mother had told me to do, my grandfather didn't buy me an ice-cream.

....

What Wisden means to me

As an ardent cricket follower and book collector, *Wisden Cricketers' Almanack* is a very special publication. It more than fulfils the dictionary definition of an almanack, namely 'an annual directory containing statistics and other information of either general or specialist interest'.

It is so much more than this – it provides a faithful record of the previous year's cricket, an account of the major issues facing the game and articles of great literary merit.

Everyone has their own favourite items within *Wisden* and it is these that they will turn to first. In my case the first port of call is the section dealing with my own county, Kent. This will be followed by all the other county reviews, the book reviews, obituaries, the schools section and the feature articles, especially the Five Cricketers of the Year. Other items will follow and it will take me several months to digest all the elements of *Wisden*.

The timing of the publication of *Wisden* is most propitious. Its annual appearance each April is keenly anticipated. No cricket season can be said to have truly started until the new *Wisden* has arrived. It should be considered the harbinger of a new cricket season with the redolent promise of months of fun and fellowship. In a competition akin to hearing the first cuckoo of spring, I used to compete with a friend of mine (a cricket bookseller by profession) to see who was first to spot that year's *Wisden*.

The first edition of *Wisden* that I came across was that of 1957. It gave a full account of Laker's demolition of the 1956 Australian tourists, and reading it was an enthralling experience. I was well and truly hooked and it soon found its way on to my bookshelves. Its original owner was an uncle and I don't know whether he ever missed it or not. I certainly never owned up to my act of purloinment. Ever since, it has retained a special place in my collection and it remains the only year for which I can quote the Five Cricketers of the Year without any hesitation.

The first edition that I purchased at the time of publication was that of 1966. I have followed this tradition every year since. I was only able to afford the purchase price in my schoolboy and student days owing to my good fortune in having an April birthday.

I have always considered April to be the ideal month for any cricketer to have their birthday. It is interesting to note that the price of the 1966 Almanack was 27 shillings and sixpence. On the basis that this year's publication is available at around £30, this represents a price increase of some 2082% over 47 years. An impressive rate of inflation!

Since that first purchase I have been fortunate enough to build up a complete collection of *Wisdens* – not all originals, alas. My collection is made up as follows:

1864-1878 – Third facsimile editions (1991)
1879-1899 – Willows reprints as published
1900-1937 – Originals, rebound in red leather
1938-1965 – Originals, a mixture of limp covers and hardbacks
1966 onwards – Original hardbacks as published.

They are all well-thumbed and much cherished. For some inexplicable reason the copies for 1967 and 1976 appear particularly well worn. The arrival of a new *Wisden* each year with a width of around two inches means that space has to be made to accommodate it. This is no easy matter with my existing collection already occupying around of 21.7 feet of shelf space.

As every collector will testify, there is great fun to be had in building up a collection of *Wisdens.* Such a process will be a lengthy and expensive one. Much of my collection was acquired in a piecemeal fashion with one or two copies being acquired at a time from specialist book dealers and secondhand bookshops.

The satisfaction to be gained from acquiring a *Wisden* at a good price from the latter is especially memorable. Regretfully this is becoming a distant memory as the book trade became more acquainted with the true value of *Wisdens.*

The Phillips auction of May 1980 (when Sir Pelham Warner's collection of *Wisdens* 1864-1963 sold for an, at the time, staggering and much-publicised sum of £7,800) was a watershed event in this respect, with the unfortunate consequence that there was a general marking-up of the prices of *Wisdens* regardless of their rarity.

Wisden for me and for many others, despite the march of technology, is still the ultimate reference work for cricketing matters. It is a source of so much information and entertainment.

The danger is that when referring to *Wisdens* in order to check or establish a fact, one can be so easily sidetracked. While browsing, the temptation to get sidetracked can be so overwhelming that after several hours of perusing something that has caught your eye, you end up forgetting the original reason for the consultation.

The annual appearance of *Wisden* has never disappointed me. Cricket is fortunate indeed that its history has been so admirably recorded in such a worthy publication. Few, if any other, sports can make such a proud boast. As a former judge of the MCC/Cricket Society Book of the Year competition, I feel that a strong case could be made out for *Wisden* being worthy of that title every year.

It is an essential part of each spring, and every cricket collection or library. Long may it continue.

....

A collector's journey
Unlike me, my father was a good cricketer who was, just once, invited to play for Dorset in the Minor Counties Championship in the early 1950s.

They were different times, and his employers wouldn't agree to pay him for the two days that he needed, so he had to decline the invitation. It was not repeated, so there is no A. R. Chandler listed in the 1953 edition of *Wisden* under those who 'also batted' for Dorset, except in my mind's eye, of course.

After the war, dad had spent two years in what was then known as Ceylon, on National Service, and playing a great deal of cricket. While he was there he picked up a 1948 *Wisden,* and he continued to buy the Almanack every year up to and including the 1957 edition, after which he stopped, apparently because he and my mother were saving up in order to buy a house and start a family. I was never terribly impressed with that as an excuse, although as I have matured I have acquired a deeper understanding of his predicament.

I was born in 1960, an event of such significance in his life that you might have expected him to celebrate by purchasing that year's edition. He didn't, but, to my eternal irritation, he did choose to mark the beginning of my younger brother's innings by purchasing the 1962 edition.

When challenged about this, he always claimed that particular acquisition was in fact inspired by his beloved Hampshire's maiden County Championship title in 1961. Secretly, I believed him, but never let on in the hope that the missing volumes might one day appear in order to make up for the perceived slight.

They never did, although some consolation was gained from his decision in 1966 to resume his annual purchase, something he did each year from then until just before his far too early death in 1989.

As a child I pored over those *Wisdens* for hours. I copied out scorecards and read the narrative content time and again. If I had a pound for every time I read Neville Cardus's article in the 1951 edition, I would think that even now I would be able to afford a full set. Long passages of the piece are still ingrained on my memory.

There was also a time when I could recite, without so much as a pause, let alone a stumble, every word and number from page 174 of the 1948 edition, so awed was I by that list of the achievements of Denis Compton, Bill Edrich and Jack Robertson in that remarkable summer of 1947.

I also used to play with all the numbers and carry out my own statistical analyses of what the book contained. I was numerate from an early age, no doubt in part thanks to *Wisden*. That said, I did not and do not have any great mathematical bent, which perhaps explains why I was able to prepare what I considered to be a wholly convincing argument in favour of the proposition that the twenty greatest players in the history of the game were all Lancastrians. I do wish I'd kept that exercise book, but sadly it has not been seen for the best part of forty years, and the methodology is long forgotten.

Once I reached my late teens, the hold that cricket had on me loosened, temporarily as it turned out, and I started to acquire other interests, and pursuing a bit of leather across a patch of green gave way to chasing other things. Looking back, even with my limited playing ability I still caught more cricket balls than I did young ladies, but I suppose that is a phase we all have to go through.

The sacrifices that my parents made for me, which resulted in my getting a decent education, eventually bore some fruit, and by 1985 I was a working man, drawing a salary, albeit a very modest one. But I still had enough money left over after keeping myself entertained, so I decided it was about time I bought a *Wisden,* and in April 1986 I did so, and I have bought a copy every year since.

That year, and again in 1987, 1988 and 1989, I let my dad read my copies. I have to say he treated them with rather more care than I had treated his, something we used to laugh about a great deal as his health deteriorated, and I regularly used to tease him about what he was ultimately prepared to accept was his greatest parenting 'fail', those missing volumes from the late '50s and early '60s.

My dad passed away peacefully in the autumn. It was an odd day. We knew he was going, but the end was rather sudden, and due to work commitments I couldn't be at his side when he breathed his last. For the first time ever I did not spend that Saturday afternoon following the football, but later found out that my team of 'southern softies', who were always awful away from home, managed to knock six past Swansea at the old Vetch. I drove home the next day and joined my mother and brother in the old family home, and we started making the necessary 'arrangements'.

On the Monday I was looking at my dad's old *Wisdens,* and concluding that the state I had left them in meant that none before 1975 were in any way collectable, the 1948 in particular rather resembling a three-dimensional jigsaw puzzle, it was in so many pieces. "Come on, Martin, this is no time to be reading those" was my mother's gentle comment to me. I agreed, but something had got into me and I felt a sudden urge to acquire the missing volumes. I rang the local secondhand bookshop, always an interesting place to visit, and was told that the proprietor had just acquired a run of *Wisden* from 1891 to 1969 and, if I hurried, I could have first refusal. They were, however, he added in sombre tones, £2,000, and he "wouldn't be able to do much on the price".

Largely as a result of my banter with my dad in his final months, I had already given some thought to acquiring the missing volumes, and had decided that I would like to acquire a set going back to 1946. I had also had a think about prices, and got a catalogue from one of the dealers. I wasn't sure, but £2,000 sounded like a decent deal from what I knew, so I got in the car and drove off. I didn't have £2,000, and with a new baby of my own couldn't possibly justify the expense, but I desperately wanted to look at the books.

When I got to the shop the owner greeted me like a long-lost friend, even though he wouldn't have known who I was until I introduced myself. He was clearly hoping for a sale. The fact that he locked the door when he knew who I was I found unnerving, but he must have spotted my discomfort and quickly told me the books were upstairs. I will never forget that staircase. It would still have been rickety if it hadn't had piles of books on most of the steps, and I kept my eyes firmly on my feet as I negotiated them, and marvelled at the way that, no doubt as a result of his familiarity with the territory, the owner skipped up them like a mountain goat.

Once in the inner sanctum, I was directed to a large box which I opened tentatively. I presume I succeeded in keeping a lid on my emotions, but the effort required to contain my amazement and delight was a real struggle.

This was not just any old run of 79 *Wisdens*. Pre 1920, most were original hardbacks, and between the wars the paper spines were all complete. The postwar books, the ones I was really after, were, as befitted the rest of the collection, in fine condition. I genuinely had no idea what they were worth, other than that they were a snip at £2,000. The way I saw it, I now had two problems. The first was where to get £2,000 from, but that was easy because I had to have the books, so I was going to find it. The other was what did I do in the meantime. I had all but been invited to haggle, but my natural English reserve put me off that anyway, and the last thing I wanted was the owner making any more detailed enquiries, or putting them downstairs where anyone might see them.

I don't know how long I was in my trance-like state, but eventually I did manage to focus on the words "Are you interested?" On the basis that discretion is the better part of valour, I simply muttered that it might take me a day or two to raise the cash. He was happy with that and I floated down the stairs and out into the street. The money, it turned out, was no problem at all. My mother had clearly started to have the same thoughts as me, and offered to lend me the money as soon as she saw the look on my face, so next day I became the proud owner of a set of books which remain my pride and joy to this day.

I am an essentially cynical man when it comes to anything to do with religion, faith or the concept that the end of life means the beginning of something else. But there has never been any doubt in my mind but that my father somehow managed to bring about my acquisition of those *Wisdens,* and what is and will forever remain absolutely certain is that I think about him every time I open one of them. It will probably come as no surprise to the reader of this story that, as time has passed, I have forgiven him for the slightly deprived childhood I had to endure without the 1958-61 and 1963-65 editions.

....

1999
My wife is a wonderful woman and when it comes to my growing *Wisden* collection she is very supportive, and in the last couple of years she has taken to contacting one person in particular for which edition/s to get me next.

My wife heard from a good friend of mine that I had played for a team back in 1998, just the once, to help them out in an emergency that involved an over-indulgent stag-night and six members of the first team being unavailable to play whilst complaining of a 'dodgy pint'. Looking on my *Wisden* shelf, there was no 1999 to be found, so my wife made a call, asking the man in question if he could check if my name was in the 1999 edition.

Unfortunately I was not mentioned in *Wisden,* but she bought it nonetheless and gave it to me along with a rather jolly 1952 on Christmas Day. She also apologised that the seller had looked right through the *Wisden* but couldn't find me inside or any mention of Brigsteer cricket team in Cumbria. Those with long-suffering partners who don't appreciate *Wisden* will not understand how proud of my wife I was.

"I'm sorry, darling, but no matter how many times you look, 0-146 in 8 overs for the seconds won't be mentioned"

1965-2012

I decided to collect *Wisdens* after buying the 2006. I had often wondered what the fascination was, as a friend at work had often talked about the yellow bible. Being rather impatient, which is a trait of mine that is mostly a negative, I couldn't just be steady (patient, even) – I had to get every one back to my birth year (1964) in one full swoop.

I rang a few dealers and was given various prices but settled on someone who said not to buy the whole lot in one go but to do it gradually over time: that way I would spend less and have a chance to enjoy them. Although slightly dubious as it meant going against my impatient gene, I decided to do just that. Then I told my wife of the plan and she was fine, until packages started arriving at regular intervals. Once they arrived I would spend hours flicking through each one, and on one occasion I let a joint of beef burn to a crisp because of a fabulous 1971. The wife went mad – ranting and shouting to such an extent that I think I might have smiled slightly, and stupidly I might have said: "Have you heard of apartheid?"

"The wife says that if I persist with my Wisden buying she will leave me.
I will miss her"

How my first Wisden cost me just a pint

Cast your mind back to the very early 1970s. The Cold War was at its height, petrol was cheap and plentiful, and beer cost 1s 10d a pint – younger readers should know this was something like 9p.

I was a young man working on the subs' desk at the *Northamptonshire Evening Telegraph* in Kettering, in the days when newspapers had sub-editors (few seem to, these days). Basically, the job entailed receiving copy and pictures for publication, designing a page, working out where each item went, checking the copy for accuracy and grammar, and liaising with the printing works to ensure that all went well.

In the course of checking some copy, I had cause to go to the newspaper's archive-cum-library, a little-visited and dusty room in a quiet area of the old building. Having checked whatever I had to in the old, bound copies of the newspaper dating from some years previously, I briefly explored my surroundings only to discover, on the top shelf of a rack, a set of *Wisdens*. They were quite possibly review copies, or perhaps the old sports editor, who had signed many of the covers, wanted them for reference – after all, Northamptonshire is a first-class county, even if we've not (yet) won the championship.

At any rate, there was a run, with the earliest edition being 1928 and just four or perhaps five copies missing to what was then the present date – 1972. As I walked back to the subs' desk, a delicious thought struck me: were these old *Wisdens* wanted by the company? They appeared just to be gathering dust and, so far as I knew, no one apart from myself and whatever secretary put each year's edition on the shelf, was aware of their existence.

Back in the subs' desk, I reported my discovery to the sports editor, who confirmed that he had no idea they were stored there. "In that case," I said, greatly daring, "would you mind if I took them home?"

"Oh, we can't do that – they're the company's property," was his immediate reaction, and my heart sank. But he thought the matter over and, later the same day, said that, as their very existence was unknown until then, perhaps it would not matter if someone took them. "However," he added, "we must be fair. Perhaps some of the others would like a few?" One of my fellow subs, being an intelligent man, was a keen cricket follower – Kent, I'm sorry to say – and he put his hand up. My heart sank again. "But I don't want a collection," he added immediately. "Just give me the latest edition, and I'll be happy."

The next day, I drove to work – I usually walked – and loaded up the boot with a set of *Wisdens* dating from 1928 to 1971 inclusive. Of course, with such a start, I had to fill in the gaps. The second set of reprints came out not very long afterwards, and I bought those so that the first 15 years were covered, and I slowly acquired the rest from the usual suspects – mainly E. K. Brown, John McKenzie and Martin Wood. The final volume, 1888, had been mine since some point in the 1980s.

And the pint? Well, it would have been churlish not to have spent 1s 10d on buying a drink for the sports editor, wouldn't it?

....

Do we have kids? Really!
My wife lets me keep my *Wisdens* in a large bookcase in our lounge. She also lets me watch cricket on the TV whenever I want and she even buys me the yellow bible for Christmas and birthdays.

During the Edgbaston Ashes Test of 2005 I, probably like the entire cricket-loving nation, was transfixed by the game. As a teacher I was off for a lot of August so I was very fortunate to see most of the second, third and fourth Tests, but the Edgbaston Test sticks out. The first three days had been incredible and when England claimed the extra half hour it looked all over.

On the fourth morning I watched every ball, cringed at every shot, gasped at the near misses. I was so nervous I even poured myself a noon pint! Just as what proved to be the final over began, my wife came in to ask me where the kids were. I was speechless: "They are with you – I'm watching the cricket."

"No," she replied, "I've been out all morning. I told you that you were looking after the kids."

"How can I be looking after the kids when we are playing Australia?"

As soon as I said that I knew it was the wrong thing to say. So our three-year-old boy and his six-year-old sister were in the house – what was the problem? The problem was they had decided to make a cake. It was a children's cake, with flour, tomato ketchup, frozen peas, cat litter, cornflakes, sugar and, of course, lots and lots of milk. The kitchen looked like a war zone and I missed the last over.

....

"I bet that old bloke with the beard looked after his children properly!"

What the Almanack means to me
The following letter appeared in *The Times* on April 6, 2013.

Sir,
*Commendations to The Times on its supplement celebrating 150 years of Wisden, even if it is
not quite on the majestic scale of your special issue of May 25, 1937, marking the centenary
of MCC.*
*This was substantial enough to be reprinted as a 132-page book (including a leather-bound
edition), its genesis owing much to the happy chance that the new President of MCC was the
Hon. J. J. Astor – owner of The Times.*
*I recall with shame my initial quest for Wisden, when as a teenager in wartime Australia,
having seen only vague references to the annual, I ventured into the vast chamber of the State
Library of Victoria to inquire if they had "Wisden"?*
A rather distant librarian responded: "We have Wisden's Almanack."
That did not sound right. An almanack could have nothing to do with cricket.
*I retreated. It took peacetime sources of information to advise me that this almanack was
indeed the essential record of the Summer Game.*

That was the not very auspicious start to my relationship with *Wisden*. Thank
goodness it was to flower and flourish over the next seventy years.

It was 1949 when I acquired my first *Wisden* – the latest edition, which took
some months to reach Australia (by sea, of course), and cost me fourteen
shillings and ninepence.

It had to be ordered from a Melbourne bookseller, as such luxuries were not to
be seen in the local newsagent/ cum/ bookseller of our small Victorian country
town. It was a good issue to start with, telling the story of Bradman's
Invincibles, and recording five memorable names as Cricketers of the Year:
Hassett, Lindwall, Morris, Bill Johnston and Tallon.

I pored over the county reports, learning a great deal about domestic English
cricket which got minimal cover in *The Argus* – the Melbourne daily our family
always bought.

But I don't recall the name of Derbyshire's then captain standing out – one E. J.
Gothard. Twenty years later, he was to propose me for MCC membership
(Lord's, not Melbourne).

I certainly read closely the report on India in Australia, the 1947/48 tour that
prepared The Don for his triumphal final tour of England. Here again, I did not
note the writer: he was Leslie Smith of the Cricket Reporting Agency, later to
be an appreciated contact as press liaison officer at Wimbledon, when in 1970 I
began a stint reporting the All-England Championships.

There was then no section dealing with cricket books of the year, but later this
became much appreciated reading, as *Wisden* after *Wisden* built up on the
shelves. 1949 saw a modest boost to my collection, courtesy of a brother

working in Melbourne's biggest secondhand bookshop – and thoughtfully slipping under the counter anything of interest. Best was a 1916 *Wisden,* lacking only the front wrapper – and costing a modest seven shillings and sixpence.

I came to England in 1953 with the aim of seeing Hassett's team in Ashes action, stepping off the good ship *Oronsay* at Tilbury on Friday, March 6 – and visiting the wonderland of Foyle's next day.

Underground was an absolute Aladdin's cave of secondhand cricket books: *Wisdens* for five bob, red *Lillywhites* at half a crown, and so much more. On and off over my two years in London, I plundered those shelves as far as my modest finances would allow (wage: seven pounds a week), sending package after package of books back home.

After I returned to Australia, the pleasure of acquiring *Wisden* as it was published was lost, but I continued buying earlier editions from UK sources, most notably from that marvellous institution, Epworth Secondhand Books, in City Road. I had discovered this shrine regrettably late when in London, but manager Leslie Gutteridge continued to offer advice in amiable correspondence.

Come 1966, and I was posted to London by my newspaper group – which meant for some months separation from my books, not least *Wisden,* until it was clear that our stay would last some years, and it was worth bringing them 10,000 miles.

It was rewarding to buy *Wisden* hot off the press, season by season, until the magic year when my friendship with David Frith, founder-editor of the new *Wisden Cricket Monthly,* brought an invitation to the annual launch dinner. The entry is there in my diary for 1980: *"April 9 – 7.15 p.m. MBH at Wisden dinner, RAF Club (Piccadilly)."*

It was the first of many: hugely enjoyable evenings, when you increasingly met new friends who became old friends. And of course you got your own copy of *Wisden* – which over the years represented quite a saving.
The next step was to get my name in *Wisden* – an ambition sparked in Adelaide, when my replacement on the local afternoon paper roused my envy, as he had made it into those august pages via the record of English public school cricket. What to write? I proposed to newish editor John Woodcock that I could do a piece for 1985 marking forty years since the resumption of postwar first-class cricket. John was dubious: surely it was 1946 when the first-class game resumed? Yes – the county championship; but 1945 had brought the Victory Tests and a handful of impromptu matches, such as Under 33 versus Over 33 at Lord's in September.

So there it was in *Wisden* 1985, page 65: 'Forty Years On' by Murray Hedgcock. But there was no byline for my next contribution, in 1990 – which was just as well, as I may have made *Wisden* history by being perhaps the only contributor to be sacked. I prepared the Obituaries section – and the editor, Graeme Wright, explained firmly that I had simply not dug deep enough into the life and times of many of those recorded. It was fair comment.

But I returned, under new editor Matthew Engel: *Wisden* for 1994 brought a review, 'The Cricket Press in 1993' – reviving my byline. However, it seemed to be my fate to tread on editors' toes. In 1998, my review of the new edition was published in my Australian newspaper before the UK embargo (such matters are a major problem with the time-lag between the two countries) and brought a complaint from a competing newspaper, and a rebuke from Matthew.

I contributed nothing for some years, but was invited to most launch dinners – on one occasion, seated alongside E. W. Swanton – possibly, I suggested, on the grounds that I of all the guests was the nearest in age to the venerable scribe.

The most memorable launch came when Robert Maxwell, whose publishing company briefly produced *Wisden,* delivered a forceful but ill-informed address, and shocked the cricket writers by announcing they had better give proper publicity to the almanack or they would no longer get free review copies.

He also said *Wisden* should be produced by computerised technology (which it already was) and that its format should be the same as the quite different dimensions of Rothman's football and rugby almanacks, which he also published. Shock, horror! Fortunately, 'Captain Bob' had only three years in charge before *Wisden* moved into safer hands.

In between all this, I researched the history of the John Wisden works at Mortlake, only a couple of miles from my home, writing a three-part series in *Wisden Cricket Monthly.*

My collection came in handy when the *Daily Mail* reported Tim Rice as worried that almanacks he needed to prepare a feature article had not arrived at his London home from their country base. As Sir Tim lives just down the road, I got in touch to offer a loan, which he was pleased to accept.

After missing two or three launches, I returned happily this year to the 150th edition dinner in the splendid setting of the Long Room at Lord's, having had the fun of writing a study of the Cricket Reporting Agency which for many years provided the editorial content of the almanack.

It was a special evening also because my cricket-enthused granddaughter Georgia had her name in the new edition, listed as an entrant in the 'Writing

Competition'. I congratulated her. She had made it at seventeen; I was 54 when my name first appeared.

Meanwhile, my collecting has continued erratically for several years, but as prices rise remorselessly, I have had to be content to complete my set with a facsimile pack of the scarce first fifteen. But I do have a couple of originals of that period, which cost me nine guineas each.

As to what *Wisden* means to me: it distils the very essence of cricket, offering a fresh thrill each year, while building an increasingly valued treasure trove, consulted and enjoyed, year after year. Long may it continue.

Murray Hedgcock

....

Man of Kent
During the summer of 2004 the exploits of a young Kent player rekindled my interest in cricket. The following year I purchased the 2005 *Wisden* and was surprised by the amount of information within its pages. This led me, as a Man of Kent, to explore through the content of these almanacks the deeds of my home county. I was able to buy on the internet a run covering the '70s.

The more I read the books, the more that I found of interest within the covers. I decided to try and purchase a run of *Wisdens* covering my lifetime, and this I achieved in 2011. My collection consists of volumes from 1946 of varying condition, all of them readable. I delve into them daily, and with the yellow dust jackets they look wonderful on my bookshelves.

....

Kick-starting a Wisden collection
I got married in 1977 and with that came a mortgage and no money, but I did have a small shelf of cricket books. I remember whilst staying with relatives for a free break in Leicester looking longingly at secondhand *Wisdens* at £3.50 each.

Two years later I bought a bookshelf at auction in St Ives for £22. I kept the shelf and a few paperbacks and sold a bag of books to a local bookshop for £7. But I also kept 14 *Wisdens,* all publisher's rebind hardbacks 1924-1938.

Sadly in my ignorance I threw away the 1933, which had no cover and was in four or five blocks (if even all there). How I lived to regret that – a mere 30 years to get a softback.

Only a couple of months later I answered an advert in a local newspaper from someone selling *Wisdens.* The seller turned out to be in my village, so around I walked to see ten hardbacks in a large leather suitcase! They were the lady's late father's. She declined my – I thought very fair – offer of £15, based on my previous purchase.

A couple of weeks later my dad was having tea with us and when I related the story he berated me. Luckily I still had the phone number, so I rang and found they were still there: I had been the only respondent. Was I still interested? Yes, and I went straight round.

Dad asked if I had enough money. "Yes," says I, "£15." He handed me a £20 note with the instruction: "Don't come back without them." I am not sure what my wife said to him while I was gone, as spending money on cricket books, albeit *Wisdens,* was still a luxury.

I stuck to my guns and bought the 1950s hardbacks for £15, but the lady felt she could not let the leather case go for that.

So it started in earnest, and I am still collecting *Wisdens* and general cricket books, which are confined (just) to two rooms.

They have given me hundreds of hours of fun, and all my friends and family know that wherever we go, I have to look in the charity and secondhand bookshops.

....

Better than after-shave
Regarding my collection, my parents bought me a very good condition 1899 hardback (which I still have) for my twenty-first in 1977. I think it cost them around £70 then – not a bad investment, methinks!

....

1973
One of the joys that I get from reading *Wisden* is that it can take you back. Reading the 1973 recently conjured up a very vivid memory of being allowed to listen to the radio in bed as Rod Marsh clouted Norman Gifford for a string of sixes. Being on a farm meant bleary eyes when I got up to help dad feed the cows the next morning. The feeling of being so grown-up was a revelation. The joy you can find in simple things!

....

Huddersfield v Botham

A friend of mine was 40 last year; he is not interested in cricket, more a soccer fan. Well, he is a season ticket holder at Huddersfield Town, so I am not sure if that is soccer or not. He was telling me about the time Huddersfield were in the old First Division, but were relegated in 1972, the year that Derby County won the championship.

His one residing memory is the fact that Huddersfield beat Derby 2-1. He told me about the game, the atmosphere, the euphoria of defeating a top team, and he asked me did I have any favourite matches. I thought long and hard and had to confess that my favourite cricket memory was of Ian Botham hitting the Australian attack all over the place at Headingley in 1981.

My friend said he had the programme from the Huddersfield match and I said I had the *Wisden* from 1982 that covered the '81 series. We swopped. I read the programme in around 15 minutes. He kept my *Wisden* for a week and then bought his own. We now have a friendly race on as to who will get a *Wisden* collection back to their birth year first: as I am a year younger I have the edge.

....

A simple transaction

I spent a total of £9 buying hardback *Wisdens* for 1916, 1917 and 1941 from a bookshop in Dulwich in 1973. Looking back, I thought I was paying neither too much nor too little, and I believe the seller thought the same.

....

Caught Murray, bowled Titmus

Although I was looking at the book, it was the smell that I remember, a nice one too – inks and paper. Also, the design was different and the feel of the front cover, a bit thicker and rougher than anything else I'd experienced.

The fascinating book was a softback version of a *Wisden Cricketers' Almanack* for 1969. It was more substantial than anything else I had seen in my 14 years on the planet so far. It was special. I knew it was. I didn't need anyone to tell me so.

I would receive another one in 1973, also a birthday gift from my parent, and 34 years later, when I was given the hardback version, that gift in 2007 would ultimately lead to me setting up Goals and Wickets, so it had a big significance. All those times from my formative years as a cricket-mad kid, aspiring player, spectator, Middlesex fan and schoolboy visitor to Test matches, would come flooding back to me.

The anticipation of another exciting day at the cricket, right from the moment of getting up and seeing another hot, sunny day. Then walking across Hampstead Heath to get on the number 13 bus. The ride through Swiss Cottage and on to St John's Wood; crossing the main road to get to the gate; the click of the turnstile at the Nursery End, where years later I would play for Finchley CC against the Cross Arrows. The purchasing of a scorecard; the sight of the magnificent pavilion at the far end of the ground as I would rush to the free seats (now called the Compton and Edrich Stands); a quick look to see which side of the square the wicket had been cut to determine where I would sit.

The decision made and a seat found, the emergence of the players and the commencement of the game with all its marvellous sights and sounds, whether John Price's funny run-up, begun with that stuttering start and around a curve as if there was an invisible obstacle placed there for him to avoid, or Eric Russell with his sleeves turned up just above his wrists as he opened another Middlesex innings with the likes of Bob Gale, Mike 'Pasty' Harris who gave me some coaching at the cricket school next to my Finchley club, Tim Selwood, also a Finchley player of significant repute, or towards the end of his career, Mike Smith.

But always at some point, for many of those visits to see Middlesex play between 1964 and 1975, we'd see the bowling of Fred Titmus who looked so innocuous but who bamboozled hundreds of batsmen into thinking that this off-break they were receiving would turn back in to their bat, only to realise, a split second too late, that it was the one which went on with the arm.

A nick on the outside edge and the ball would be nestling in John Murray's gloves. JT would raise an arm, Fred would look around at the umpire: the appeal seemed co-ordinated from both ends of the wicket. The finger would be raised and off the batsman would go.

The trip to the ground, the sights and sounds of Lord's, the Middlesex players of the 1960s and 1970s, encapsulated in the sight of another dismissal by the two great Middlesex stalwarts.

Caught Murray, bowled Titmus – that's what the yellow bible means to me.

Mark Cripps (www.GoalsandWickets.co.uk)

....

Literacy Legacy of "the Little Wonder" still standing tall

From all accounts, John Wisden was a man of modesty and charm who would never have believed that one day the sporting world's most noted book of reference would be that which bears his name.

He died in 1884, 34 years after achieving lasting fame as a cricketer by bowling all ten men in an innings, playing for the North against the South at Lord's, a feat still without parallel in first-class cricket. Of all bowling records only Jim Laker's 19 wickets in a Test match is more unlikely to be equaled than the Little Wonder's all ten.

Wisden's bowling that day at Lord's is a source of endless fascination. We are told that his pace was "fast and ripping" (Wisden was only 5ft $4_{1/2}$ in and 7st, and over-arm bowling had yet to be legalized) and that "without exaggeration, his balls turned a yard from the off." By any reckoning that is a lethal combination and it is, I am sure, just as it must have been at the time. Lord's was still a meadow, not a lawn; sheep grazed there and no pitch had ever had a mower taken to it.

The game never has been what it was. Yet, year after year, the same issues and uneasinesses have recurred in *Wisden's* Notes by the Editor, which first appeared in 1901. In this annual encyclical of 100 years ago, for example, Australia's former demon bowler, F.R.Spofforth, is reported as suggesting a bonus of two runs be given to the fielding side for every maiden over bowled. Although Sydney Pardon, *Wisden's* Editor from 1891 until 1925, calls it "an absurd proposition", it shows how today's restlessness was yesterday's too.

No family ever did more to establish *Wisden's* reputation than the Pardon family. They founded the Cricket Reporting Agency (CRA) which put the almanack together from 1887 until the 1960s. A collection of good companions, several of whom I came to know as colleagues in the press box, they would head for Fleet Street, spend the morning working on *Wisden*, go to the pub for lunch and return afterwards to continue what for them was more an enjoyable challenge than a chore. In the next year's edition, a page would be set aside for "errata", which could probably have run to a second, so infinite is the scope for error and relatively random were the means of communication.

When I became Editor in 1980, the Prestons, Hubert and Norman, had served *Wisden* as faithfully and for almost as long as the Pardons. Although Sydney Southerton, who edited the editions of 1934 and 1935 and was long a stalwart of the CRA, had covered the England tour to Australia in 1928-29, Norman Preston was the first editor to go overseas with an England side while in office. Three years after taking over from his father, he came to Australia in 1954-55. A Pickwickian figure, he was reporting the tour for Reuters and the Press Association, and singing in the cathedral choirs whenever he could.

Whereas the first editor's main aim was to fill the pages–so much so that the changes of the moon, the rules of bowls, the winners of the Derby and the dates of the Battle of Bosworth all got a touch–by 1980, the almanack had reached bursting point. The problem of choosing the Five Cricketers of the Year was as nothing compared to what to leave out. The 1933 *Wisden*, the first I came to know off by heart, ran to 1,031pages. Today it tops 1,500. Such was the hold the 1933 *Wisden* had over me that one of my school reports that year warned it was high time Hillard & Botting (aka Holland & Blotch), the primary Latin textbook, got a look-in.

Just as in the days of the Pardons and the Prestons, so in the 1980s editing the great work was very much a team effort, with the regular staff meetings held not in and around London but in a Hampshire village.

In the six years for which I did it, it had the feel of a cottage industry. Each year there are something like 100 contributors, all of them gratified to be asked, or so one liked to think. It took some persuasion to get Sir Donald Bradman on board, but his declared affection for *Wisden* swung it. When, briefly, Robert Maxwell owned the publishing rights, he got the sort of reaction to which he was quite unaccustomed upon saying to Sir Gubby Allen, sitting next to him at the annual dinner, that he had it in mind to change the shape of the book. It has, in fact, never altered.

In their wisdom, with every kind of statistic now instantly available online, recent editors have felt the need for *Wisden* to become more literary, to stand out as much for its writing as for its facts and figures. The miscellanea of old are still there, but relating exclusively to cricket. If sometimes in the most esoteric of ways. There will be some 20 feature articles this year rather than the five in my last as Editor.

The modern *Wisden* is a marvel of accuracy and inclusiveness. And nothing seems to stop the price of a complete set of originals from going through the roof. In 1954, one could be bought for £250. Something similar has gone within the past two years for £120,000. With "the Little Wonder's" signature in the 1864 edition, it could have been up there with a first folio of Shakespeare. Collecting this "harbinger of spring" from years ago has become an investment no less than a hobby

John Woodcock (Wisden Editor, 1981-86)

The Times, April 5 2013, 'Reproduced by kind permission of The Times.'

....

Priceless

I am in my ninetieth year and I do have many memories of cricket. I am no poet, but I have wonderful images that conjure up the colours and shadows of Lord's on Test match day or the scent of the sea air at Hove, the greeting of old friends and the making of new ones. And I can fondly relive those inspiring days and warm friendships with a flick through a *Wisden*. What joy!

> When life gets tough and stress is high
> And you're not hitting your right chords
> The solution lies in North-West 8
> With a blissful day at Lord's

....

What Wisden Means to Me

I have been collecting *Wisden*s for quite a long time. I 'borrowed' my first one, 1967, from the high school library late that year when I was 12 and it has been with me on a 'long-term loan' ever since! The purists would probably say it is a bit of a 'scruffy' collection, with many good copies, some arguably not so good and nothing matching. However, I don't care what they look like because I buy them to read – not sit on a shelf and look attractive. Apart from my wife and children, they are my pride and joy.

....

Thank you..

William Abbotsley

Peter Ackerman

Philip Anderson

Sam Andrews

Alistair Banks

Derek Barnard

Paul Barratt

Michael Bawes

Michael Baws

David Beecroft

Bob Bond

Lawrence Booth

Chris Boothby

Geoff Boscawen

Martin Briggs

Tom Brockwell

Glen Browne

Dominique Bryne

Simon Burrowes

Frank Camilleri

Michael Carter

Bob Cavendish

Martin Chandler

Mike Clarke

Robert Cleveland

Ken Cook

Mark Coulson

Mark Cripps

Tony Davies

Ian Derbyshire

John Dickson

Norman East

Graham Elliott

Keith Evans

Chris Finch

Ric Finlay

Malcolm Forbes

Graham Foster

David Fox

David Frith

Lorraine Furmedge

Matt Gartside

Timothy Gibson

Ian Grey

Stephen Gubb

Aidan Haile

Nick Hall

Lady Angela Haselhurst

Paul Heaney

Alan E Hebiton

Murray Hedgcock

Mrs Pam Henderson

Andy Hogg

Simon Hull

Harry Jackson

Victoria Jackson

David Jenkins

Robert Jones

Don Lambert

Phil Lambert

Christopher Lane

Fred Larkin

Mark Lawley

Richard Lawrence

Thank you..

Mark Leader
Brian Leatham
Anton Leigh
Tim Lewis
Richard Ley
Graeme Lilley
Ed Lockwood
Steven Lynch
Duncan Mathieson
David Matthews
Alan E Moore
Christopher Moore
Niall Moore
Peter Motum
Ian Murrie
Lisa O'Neil
Stewart Ord
Tim Ord
Dan Parkinson
Stuart Parsons
Steve Pickard
Ken Piesse
John Pratt
Matthew Price
Adrian Pye
David Quinn
Andrew Renshaw
Jonathan Rice

John Richardson
Pete Roberts
Gordon Rother
Brian Rowe
Richard Saltmarsh
Tony Shaw
John Sherwood
Derrick Simpson
David Sleight
Graeme Sterat
Colin Stirling
John Stockwell
John Swain
Mrs B Tennyson
Dennis Thomas
Richard Trainor
Paul Turnbull
Michael Waby
Roy Watts
John Welch
Alec Whewell
Graeme White
Una White
David Wild
James Wilkinson
Robbie Wilton
John Woodcock
Alison Wring

"It has been a pleasure putting this book together but I could not have done it without the contributions and the support, help and encouragement from those above. If I have omitted anyone then I apologise profusely"

Bill Furmedge, July 2013